To R[...]

With best wishes.

GIBBON'S YEARS

Jack Macdonald

GIBBON'S YEARS

Jock Macdonald

Matador
Unit E2 Airfield Business Park,
Harrison Road, Market Harborough,
Leicestershire. LE16 7UL
Tel: 0116 279 2299
Email: books@troubador.co.uk
Web: www.troubador.co.uk/matador
Twitter: @matadorbooks

ISBN 978 1 80313 293 8

British Library Cataloguing in Publication Data.
A catalogue record for this book is available from the British Library.

Printed and bound in Great Britain by 4edge Limited
Typeset in 11pt Adobe Garamond Pro by Troubador Publishing Ltd, Leicester, UK

Matador is an imprint of Troubador Publishing Ltd

"*Rich in recollection and reflection, a memoir to delight and disturb.*"

Allan Massie CBE, novelist and commentator.

"*Most engaging and enjoyable, challenging us with clarity and conviction on the political urgency of tackling climate change now.*"

Tony Stoller CBE, University of Bournemouth

"*This entertaining, frank account confirms for me the importance of archaeology's long-term vision of the planet.*"

Simon Stoddart, Dept. of Archaeology, Cambridge

CONTENTS & CHRONOLOGY

PROLOGUE

"If a man were called to fix the period in the history of the world during which the condition of the human race was most happy and prosperous, he would, without hesitation, name that which elapsed from the death of the Emperor Domitian to the accession of Commodus." (AD 98–180) Edward Gibbon, *Decline and Fall of the Roman Empire*, Ch.3 (written c. AD 1785)

"Look back over the past with its changing empires that rose and fell and you can foresee the future too." Emperor Marcus Aurelius, *Meditations* (written c. AD 175)

"The Child is Father of the Man." Wordsworth, *Poems in Two Volumes* (1807)

"We have to make sure, above all, that our mind is not halved by a horizon." Amartya Sen, *Identity and Violence* – last line (Allen Lane, 2006)

This is not an autobiography. Nor is it a memoir. It is (to use the modern term) a kind of lens. And the focus of the lens? The Second World War and the second half of the twentieth century. But the lens could well be distorted, and so it needs some description and explanation of its development, which are: growing up in the 1940s and living in the second half of the twentieth century as a well-educated, flawed, ordinary, white, middle-class, middle-salaried, tolerably well-connected, quite lucky someone with the time to think. Perhaps it also concerns those many other people who looking back over the years say how fortunate they have been to have lived in that period in the Western World. Compared to the first fifty years of the twentieth century and the mass privations of the nineteenth, it was a golden age of technical and social progress. The lens may seem more focussed and straightforward than it should be; I have not included many of the complications, both good and bad, that unsurprisingly have involved and absorbed a person now in his early eighties. But when the lens starts to focus on the introductory years of the twenty-first century, the increasingly turbulent and muddy conditions of the time, not to mention the contemporary nature of events, have made a steady aim much more difficult, even if at times the focus is sharper.

Though the last fifty years of the twentieth century can be compared to those famous years back in the second century AD to which Edward Gibbon refers, there were, nevertheless, intimations of calamity just over the horizon, intimations sensed by some early on, by others only recently, and by some, even now, hardly at all. I was sensing them early in my adulthood, for which I take no credit; my DNA and upbringing are entirely responsible. The coming calamity is the climate crisis, for which the simplest measurements are the growth in the world's human population, the gathering thickness of the blanket of CO_2 enveloping our planet, and the resulting increase in extra heat to which more and more humans and species of every kind will be subject. As I recount the almost blessed years that I and others have experienced, I shall from time to time give data for the oncoming calamity, randomly placed with no reference to the content of the story: they are, mere numbers for the world's population, particles per million for the blanket of CO_2, and degrees in centigrade for the increase in the world's temperature since AD 1800. In fact, 1800 is the base for all the numbers. So, for instance, in 1800 there were some 1 billion of us humans in the world; now there are 8 billion. In 1800, particles per million of CO_2 amounted to about 280 and had stood near that number for several millennia; now there are 415. As for heat, it is now 1.2 degrees Celsius hotter than it was in 1800, all because of that blanket. There has never been a thicker blanket nor a higher overall ambient temperature in the world for all the 300,000 years of human existence.

But first a thought from Claire Tomalin. In her *A Life of My Own*, written when she was eighty-four, she expresses well what I have come to recognise: "One thing," she says, "I have learnt *[through writing her book]* that while I used to think I was making individual choices I see clearly that I was following trends and general patterns of behaviour which I was about as powerless to resist as a migrating bird or a salmon swimming upstream." This is true of me and, I think, everyone. At a time of great change like the one we have reached in the early twenty-first century, the question is: Which individuals and groups will be best suited in their "trends and general patterns" to dealing with the rest of this half-century?

To whom then shall I dedicate this little lens, such as it is? To those, I think, who have had to put up with me as a family man, which is an important part of the lens. They might even want to change what I have written. Their names? Jane, my present wife, is one. Felicity, my former wife, another. Then there are my daughters: Carlina, sadly no longer, and Alessia, vibrant and thoughtful. Finally, my two grandchildren, Otto and Minna, for whom particularly, like it or not, this has been written. For their future will be challenging.

Part 1: FASHIONING THE LENS

CONSCIOUSNESS of SELF:
The Second World War in India,
1942–1945

1 The Himalayas

I remember those mountains, vividly. They were only eighty miles away. They were massive and stretched right across the northern horizon, shining a dazzling white in the afternoon sun and fading slowly into a steely grey in the evening twilight. I knew their names: Hathi Parvat, Nanda Ghunti, and my favourite, Trisul, and then, hiding behind them and somewhat to the right so that I was never quite sure that I saw it, the sharp triangle of Nanda Devi – the mountain of the Bliss-Giving Goddess.

I was four years old and the mountains were the backdrop and context to whatever I did, wherever I went and whoever I was with. They were there when my sister and I woke in the morning and again when we went to bed in the evening. We saw them when we ran around our large, sandy garden swerving past borders that overflowed with

English flowers: sweet peas, pansies, chrysanthemums and snapdragons. Brilliantly coloured butterflies fluttered in and out of them, blue and red, white and orange, and tiny black-and-yellows. Those last were my favourites. I used to creep up on them; and when they folded their wings I would catch them between my thumb and forefinger. Then I inspected them, and let them go.

Above the house and garden there rose a red sandy cliff, Joan Mary's domain, her castle, out of bounds to me. Beyond the garden on two sides there was jungle. Undulating out towards the Himalayas were ridge upon ridge of dark green rhododendrons. And in front of the house there was a pine forest and a spring of water that turned into a tiny, bubbling stream. There was also a walled kitchen garden often raided by monkeys. My mother worried that they might carry me away. Beyond the kitchen garden and on the other side of a shallow valley lay a small, dun village. And if the breeze was right we could smell the aromas of burning cow dung and curries. This was where I became aware of myself in a context.

That included some danger, not so much from the jungle but it seemed from humans. My mother slept with a pistol under her pillow. My father was in Ceylon, in Colombo, building a harbour. There was a war on, against the Japanese. Some Indians, they said, were wanting to join them. Every so often old retired General Fitzgerald would come to visit us and take afternoon tea. He was wanting to make sure we were safe. Or perhaps he just liked talking to my mother. He usually came with his pretty ADC, Mary Lane. I remember thinking she was pretty in her uniform and reddy-golden hair under her cap. She was his driver and she drove a rather exciting car that had a coupé in the back where two people could sit in the open as the car sped along. Not that we ever went in it, except when it was parked in front of the house.

We were not totally isolated. Up the road a longish walk away was the hotel where we had stayed when we first came up to Ranikhet for the hot season. Then when Dad went to Ceylon we stayed on, moving to the bungalow for the rainy season (when in fact that year the rains hardly came), through the colder weather when I first saw ice, then the spring and another hot season. There was a church, which I can hardly remember apart from going there on Christmas Day. And one or two other fatherless families were living within walking distance. But there was no school. Mum taught JM, who was nine at the time. Their lessons were in the sunlit garden. I used to listen in, but I can't remember any talk of numbers, only of plays, Puck, and poetry. I liked repeating the lines from *A Midsummer's Night Dream*:

"You spotted snakes with double tongue, /Thorny hedge-hogs be not seen.

Newts and blind-worms do no wrong/ Come not near our fairy queen."

I was sent to "school" at the McGregors', who lived nearby. I hated it and was taken away after two days. Joan Mary was mad about boats. She got me to help her dig a life-size dinghy out of the sandy surface of the garden. We pretended to row across the ocean, or sometimes we played doctors and nurses. I was given a teddy bear for my fourth birthday, sent all the way from Dad in Colombo. He was called Stubbins and he kept me busy. He also slept in my bed, in a bedroom shared with JM. Late one night, when the pine logs were still burning in our bedroom fireplace, we thought we heard something padding past our window. Next morning we did see pugmarks in the sand, but they were too small to be a tiger's. But they did not belong to one of the hyenas that we could often hear barking in the night.

Animals did provide some danger. Apart from the monkeys about which my mother was so worried, JM and I occasionally rode ponies. I was more or less fastened to an old piebald called Tommy led by an attendant, but JM rode a frisky mare, so frisky indeed that it bit her. I was very worried by that. Even more worrying was an occasion when she had dismounted, was walking backwards when I saw a little snake in her path. I knew about little snakes. They could be deadly kraits. "Stop!" She did, and the snake wriggled away. More numerous and annoying were leeches that lived near the tiny stream. And so I was not allowed to play there. But the deer that came out of the forest were beautiful. One afternoon, when we had risen from our compulsory rest, we saw Mum sitting very still in the bright sunlight under the blossom of the apricot tree. She was looking intently at a small spotted deer that had come within feet of her. Then the deer saw us and turned away to trot back into the pine forest.

2 Travel by Train

After our second hot season we left Ranikhet. A bus, empty apart from one or two wooden seats, arrived in front of the bungalow. Furniture, tin trunks and canvas bags were piled into it, and onto the roof. Soon we were zig-zagging down a road overhung with trees, their leaves bright in the sunshine. Monkeys bounced on and off the roof, even more so when the bus stopped for repairs. Apparently, steam was coming out of the engine. The driver and his assistant asked Mum if she had soap to plug a hole in the radiator. The soap was found, and the hole was plugged. The monkeys were shooed away and we proceeded down to the open plain, to Kathgodam where a train was waiting in a siding.

In the bright late-afternoon sunshine we climbed on to the train. I was very excited. We were going on a long journey, right across India. And the compartment with its bunks, polished wooden walls and a toilet that even flushed when you pulled a handle, this was all strange and wonderful. We were even going to sleep in it. And sleep we did. Before I knew it, we had arrived in Bareilly station, in time for a breakfast of scrambled eggs in the station restaurant. Then boarding another train we travelled across the North of India past industrial towns and factories belching smoke. I could not take my eyes off the scenes passing by. Eventually we arrived after nightfall at Benares where we were due to change trains. We stood patiently on the platform until a huge locomotive with a huge headlight came in, rumbling and hissing to a stop. We found our compartment. It was minute. JM and I slept in a top bunk and Mum was below. Somehow we reached Calcutta in the afternoon of the next day.

There were crowds of people in Howrah station; and outside, where we caught a taxi, the streets were littered with people either dead or sleeping. But we stayed the night with a friendly couple who owned an apartment reached by a lift. The bathroom was very modern. There were chrome fittings and a gas geyser that heated up the water. It seemed comfortable. The next day we went to a station that seemed different, again through streets littered with people lying on the ground. This time we caught a train to Amyngong where in the late afternoon we boarded a ferry to take us across a huge river. It was called the Brahmaputra. Once on the other side we took a taxi from Gauhati up through foggy hills to our destination, Shillong, the capital of Assam. It was in a war zone where Dad had been posted, away from building his harbour in Colombo. Apparently, Mum had with great difficulty and a lot of determination received permission to be in this war zone, despite the Japanese army having advanced right through Burma up to the Indian frontier. They were laying siege to Imphal and Kohima, where British and Indian troops had halted their advance – at least for the time being. All this I was only slightly aware of.

3 Assam

What I was aware of was rain and mud. It had hardly rained in Ranikhet, but Assam was a different matter. The mud was everywhere – wet, slimy mud, churned up by army lorries, huge industrial pipes and lots of soldiers wearing different badges. There were the British with unfathomable accents, Yanks, Indians, and very black Africans. My favourite army shoulder badge was a big black elephant, the badge of the Africans fighting with the British. The Fourteenth Army in which Dad was serving as a Royal Engineer had a rather soppy badge. It looked like the picture on the Dettol bottle that was kept in our bathroom.

Our bathroom was a dark, cold room with a very faint blue electric light, designed not to be seen by enemy aircraft. It was beside a room in which we all slept, even Dad when he was on one very short leave. We were in a boarding house called Brookside; it took its name from a torrent that hurtled past the bottom of the untidy garden. Brookside was where officers and their families lived. Bachelor officers occasionally got drunk. One night JM and I were woken up by someone in our room, and it wasn't Mum. This person was stumbling about, bumping into things. Very bravely JM switched on a light and in the gloom we could see this American officer. Somehow JM guided him out of the room into the garden.

On Dad's brief leave I helped him build a culvert to drain a large puddle outside our room. When an aeroplane with a curiously divided body went overhead he explained that it was not a Japanese one because the enemy did not have many planes. Dad was not with us for Christmas, nor for my birthday when I got into trouble for getting into a car and letting the brake off. JM got into even worse trouble because she looked at all her presents before Christmas and almost immediately her right leg went lame. She was taken to hospital but returned a few days later. There was talk of polio. But she thought God was punishing her for being so naughty. Soon after that she went to school at Loreto convent. She went by the school bus and one day came back very excited because the bus had lost a wheel, which all the children saw rolling ahead. The driver had stopped the bus, made the children get out, and went to fetch the wheel to fix it back on.

I too, some months later, went to school on the bus. But that did not last long because we left Brookside to live in a bungalow on a hillside near the school. It was not as wonderful as our bungalow in Ranikhet, but it was much better than Brookside. It had two drives, which I thought was very grand, and a grassy lawn that had been a tennis court. One of the drives led up to the front of the veranda from the road below. It passed through trees where it turned very sharply. The other drive descended to a ramshackle garage above the house. It came from the same road as the one below. The road, ascending the hill, had performed a very sharp hairpin bend so that it was both above and below the house. All the land in the middle seemed to belong to us. At the side where there was no road there was a shady valley with a stream and beyond the stream, a path going up the hill with a series of steps, earning it the name of Jacob's

Ladder. Older schoolchildren, both European and Indian, walked up and down it, to go up to the convent, or, if they were boys, to Don Bosco's School for Boys.

And so there was plenty of space for me in which to rush around. We had several servants: a *mali* to look after the garden, a *pani-wallah* who was in charge of the boiler and water tanks behind the house. He used to take water from them in big carriers for us to use in our tin baths. There was our bearer, Jumra Ali, a cook who had his kitchen down the hill from the house towards the hairpin bend, and Phyllis who was my *ayah*-cum-help-in-the-house. I liked her a lot, and her daughter too, Nina, about the same age as me. Phyllis lived just beyond the kitchen in a bedroom that she kept spotless despite its mud walls and mud floors. Phyllis gave us a small ginger cat named Flopsy. A little kid goat also arrived. Nina and I tried to feed it with a bottle. It died soon afterwards. I played a lot on my own, making several expeditions under the house which was built on stilts. That area became out of bounds when I was told that snakes lived there. Out in the open I trailed a steamroller made by Dad out of tobacco tins round the wooded paths below the house, or, as I ran along, I was the pilot of a wooden aeroplane that I was given for my sixth birthday. I tried to build a model bazaar on a steep muddy slope beside and above the tennis court. I was pleased when Mum said it looked like a village on the Italian Riviera. I liked the sound of that.

During term-time, JM and I used to walk up to school in the morning, come home for lunch and then go up to school again. I learnt to read, liked arithmetic, but loved geography, particularly eskimos, igloos, and polar bears. I also liked making a model of the heroic island of Malta, concentrating on the Grand Harbour. I had a friend called Christopher who seemed to have an impressive knowledge of the world, particularly of earthquakes, probably because Assam was in an earthquake zone. And so we played "Lisbon". This entailed building a pretend city and then knocking it down. Which we often did. Near the end of the war JM took me on imaginary sea journeys back to Scotland: across the Indian Ocean, up the Red Sea, through the Suez canal, past the Holy Land and Malta and out into the Atlantic. She had done the real journey twice when she was four.

At about this time I became aware of religion. After all, I was being taught by nuns, benign black-robed nuns. But one afternoon our class was taken by a young, pretty nun in a white habit to visit a little, sunlit chapel. When we were all sitting down, she went to the altar and produced a red object. "This," she announced, "is Jesus' heart." I did not believe her. Jesus died miles away, I thought, in the Holy Land, which I had actually visited on one of our imaginary voyages. This first act of agnosticism did not, however, prevent me from kneeling on the steps leading to the top drive and praying for rain. Which duly came that evening. This was important because the monsoon rains had failed two years running and poverty-stricken Indians were desperate. The rain when it came was incredibly heavy. It thundered down on the bungalow's tin roof and poured over the front of the veranda. I rather regretted my act of prayer. It may have been influenced by the two daughters of the local Anglican vicar who had come to tea one afternoon. My mother had made sure that there were such sandwiches and cake as could be put together towards the end of a war. One of the girls said in a rather prissy voice: "This food should have been given to the poor people of Calcutta." After they had gone my mother was not happy. "Little holier-than-thous," she scoffed. But, I thought, they do have a point – I have seen people dying in the streets of Calcutta.

One overcast afternoon I experienced a horrid wriggly sensation at the bottom of my back when I was playing with my "Italian Riviera" village. Running inside, I went to the lavatory and was appalled to see that I had produced a long white worm. I was immediately taken to the hospital and put in a room on my own. I was there for three days feeling somewhat lonely without anything obvious happening to me. The only good event was when a nurse pointed out the great white mountain of Kangchenjunga, which stood many miles away. But there was another rather puzzling occasion. One day, just after lunch, an Assamese nurse took me to visit other patients: gaunt, cadaverous men, many with limbs missing. They looked disturbingly similar to the bodies in newspaper photographs of Belsen and Auschwitz. In fact these men had been rescued from Japanese prisoner-of-war camps. I remember them looking kindly at me; possibly the nurse had wanted them to see a child unaffected by war.

But the war was coming to an end. First came victory in Europe with the newspaper maps showing large black arrows converging from Europe and Russia on Germany. In Burma, though, the war was dragging on. Dad had been making roads there with the help of elephants and had taken part in the crossing of the large River Irrawaddy. It was only then that he saw any fighting because his job was to build vital communications behind the advancing army. I remember his letters describing the elephants working in the jungle, pushing huge tree trunks with their tusks to make bridges or embankments. And on one occasion a spotted leopard bounded across the road in front of his jeep. I remember letters coming from our grandparents in Scotland, the first time I became aware that such people as grandparents existed. In a war zone, letters arriving from Britain were very rare.

The war against Japan did finally come to an end. There was a huge firework display after dark on the side of the lake near Government House. The convent put on a theatrical performance about returning home by sea to England. I was dressed up as a female Puff of Wind, while my friend Drick was a male Squall. I would have much preferred to have been a squall. Dad was home more often now and our possessions began to be packed up in crates and black tin boxes painted by us with white lettering: "Wanted" or "Not Wanted on Voyage". JM had had her twelfth birthday when she and her friends played "Murder". Somehow I was a part of it and had bad dreams the following night. There was also a small earthquake and we had to be inoculated against cholera and smallpox, which made me feel very wretched. I had whooping cough too; I whooped once. The Americans organised a rodeo show with bucking broncos and clouds of dust. Parties of families went by jeep for picnics beside streams. At one of them a bright green cobra slipped silently by, through the damp grass. It was very strange sitting in the bubbling water. Sometimes my parents played golf and we children would wait on a green halfway round the course, passing the time with putting competitions until they arrived.

Now that the war was over, Americans were more and more obvious. Dad did not like them. He saw them as rivals. They had not fought in Burma but had used Assam as a base for flying troops and supplies to China over The Hump, meaning the eastern end of the Himalayas. Their general, Joseph Stillwell, according to Dad, was a show-off. His nickname was Vinegar Joe. Even worse, according to Dad, they were encouraging the Indians to leave the British Empire. "Who needs the Japanese as enemies, when your friends are the Americans," he once said. I rather agreed. My hair was given a decent cut at the Club where pink-tinted posters advertised an American film called *Little Dolly Daydream*. What a soppy film that must be, I thought to myself.

Not only did I have my hair cut before going back to Britain, but we visited the bazaar to buy new clothes for the new country, an experience I had never had until then. Perhaps most important of all in my mother's eyes, she organised Mother Columba, the gentle and impressive head of the Convent, to teach me to sing the metrical versions of Psalms 23 and 121 while she accompanied me on the piano. This was to impress my Presbyterian minister grandfather, who had been the Moderator of the General Assembly of the Church of Scotland.

4 Travel by Train and Ship

Finally, the day came and we left. On the morning of our departure, JM and I walked down our lower drive to the road, and there we found and talked to our little cat. She was at the bottom of a conical basket covered by muslin with a hole in it. She was mewing piteously, so we fed her with monkey nuts. Then, sometime later, a car took us down roads that curved and swerved between misty mountain forests and tea plantations until we finally reached the Brahmaputra. We crossed it, once again on a foggy evening. The ferry was crowded, noisy and smelly and went so slowly that I could not believe that it was moving. We boarded a night train for Calcutta that took most of the next day to reach its destination. This time we stayed in a grand hotel. We went shopping for clothes suitable for a Scottish winter: jumpers, shoes, and raincoats. We lunched in the British Club and swam in its indoor pool. Swam? I sat bewildered on the edge dangling my legs in the water. The next evening as it was getting dark we arrived in a taxi at Howrah station. Once again there were bodies lying all over the platforms and beggars jostling us for money. When we found our compartment my mother insisted that Joan Mary and I pull mad faces to make quite sure that the compartment was ours and ours alone.

I slept on a bottom bunk and woke far earlier than the others; the train was rumbling over a large river on a rackety bridge. I kept my nose pressed against the glass of the window watching farms and villages and buffaloes and camels as they went by. At Allahabad (I remember the name) the train stopped. The station was as crowded as Howrah but in the daylight we could look around. There was a conjuror doing his tricks and another man playing his pipe to a cobra rearing out of a basket. To my dismay, when the train started again it went backwards! I could not bear the thought of going backwards, back to Shillong. I wanted to go forward. Which we did, but backwards. Another night on the train.

The next day it was very hot. From time to time the train stopped in sidings; the passengers stepped down from their compartments to walk to the restaurant for breakfast and lunch. Late in the afternoon we reached Deolali. Deolali had for a long time been a transit camp for the British Army in India. It was a bare hundred miles from Bombay. And there we waited for three weeks until we could board a suitable troopship to take us back to Britain.

It was extremely hot. The sun had no pity. But an outdoor swimming pool did. I almost learnt to swim by jumping as far as I could into the pool where my father waited to gather me up. At night mosquitoes were ready to pounce in swarms, but we were protected by mosquito nets of which I had a dim memory from some years earlier. We lived in a hut, but dined in a very large communal hall. In the evening I played in a pile of old tyres outside our quarters. At one point a bunch of boys tried to bully me off it, claiming it to be their castle. I was very upset. As a result my father showed me how to box. I was pleased by that.

Other families in transit began to leave for the troopships in Bombay. We seemed to have been forgotten. But at last we were off, in a train that had a corridor, a sophistication that I had never experienced. It was a very fast train, roaring over the watershed of the Western Ghats and rushing down deep, green valleys on the other side. If Deolali was hot, Bombay was hotter and stiflingly humid. Our ship, the *Samaria*, a Cunarder converted into a troopship, was packed. Women and children were separated from men. The cabin in which I found myself had once been three double cabins, but now held eighteen women and several children. This was not the excitement that I had anticipated. I was very unhappy until my father somehow persuaded someone that I would be better off in his single cabin, a space that now held seven grown-up men and me. What do I remember of the voyage? Bony kippers for breakfast. The ship's wake, as we steamed south over the Indian Ocean. Rounding Aden. Being passed in the Red Sea by a battleship, the *King George the Fifth*. Everybody cheered wildly and sang "Rule Britannia". I have a vision of the sailors lining the battleship in a salute. Then early one morning, Suez. And men in small boats jabbering away, trying to sell their wares. Most memorable of all, the ship ran aground in the middle of the next night. It was a transatlantic liner and did not fit easily into the Suez Canal. All the passengers were told to leave their cabins and go out on deck: old women and children, men in pyjamas, ladies with curlers in their hair, and soldiers looking rather rough. We all had to do it. "It" was to rush from one side of the ship to the other, to rock it off the sand. The manoeuvre was successful.

We passed Port Said the next day at teatime. As we began to plough into the rough Mediterranean sea, for the first time since Ranikhet I felt cold. We all felt cold. In the following days we huddled under blankets on the deck, with Dad showing me how to make model ships out of match boxes; oil tankers were the easiest, and liners easier than battleships. "We won't need battleships much longer, will we, Dad?" Dad did not seem optimistic. "The enemy is now Russia." And I could remember those maps in newspapers six months earlier that showed big arrows converging on Germany, not just from the West, but from the East as well. We passed through the sunny straits of Gibraltar with a shoal of dolphins leaping and gambolling in front and beside us, and then we threw our Indian topi sun hats into the long, rolling oncoming swell of the Atlantic.

One night, two or three days later, we docked in Liverpool. I had just recovered from a small bout of sickness. We disembarked the next day while it was still dark. It was also foggy. We had been given American K rations for the train journey to Scotland. Liverpool was a pile of rubble. All we could do was to gaze at it in a state of bemusement, as we wiped away the steam from the carriage windows. The train travelled north and a weak winter sun appeared and took us over the border past Carlisle. I was interested in Carlisle, because the friendly steward who looked after our cabin came from Carlisle. His name was Wattie and he told me to look out for his home town. The train came to a halt in the Caledonian Station at the west end of Princes Street in Edinburgh. On the platform in the dark station my father stopped to talk to a couple of soldiers. Though they were supposed to be speaking English, for all I knew they were speaking some weird form of Hindustani, so full of glottal stops were their sounds. They for their part took me to be a little Indian boy because I spoke with an Indian accent. A taxi took us along Princes Street from the Caledonian to Waverley Station. On our right a great mass loomed through the twilight fog. Edinburgh Castle? Yes, Edinburgh Castle. I must have seen a newspaper picture of it when we were in Shillong. Our destination was North Berwick on the coast of the Firth of Forth. We were due to stay in the Elphinstone Hotel. The McCabe family, who owned it, were very welcoming and gave us scalding stone hot water bottles to keep us warm in bed.

5 Grandparents and Cousins

Next morning Joan Mary could not wait to hustle me out across the damp grass of the golf course to see the sea. This was her heaven: back in Scotland. The sea was flat and grey, stretching right out to the horizon. There was a wrecked fishing boat lying on the grey, wet sand.

The Elphinstone Hotel was now closing for the winter. The McCabes had kept it open especially for us, but they had not expected our voyage back from India to be so delayed. We moved up the hill from the seaside to stay at a guest house called Ardvulin. Our time there was memorable to me for several reasons. Above all, it being now December, daylight hardly existed; it was almost perpetual night. I also celebrated my seventh birthday there – and Christmas. My rather unlikely birthday treat was a visit to the ballet at the

Empire Theatre in Edinburgh. It was in fact a great treat. I loved it, even though I cannot now remember the details. A cousin, Jean, also came to it. Four years older than JM, she seemed a very grown-up girl. For Christmas evening we went on a shiveringly cold and uncomfortable journey by car along the coast road with the lights of Fife flashing across the Firth of Forth. But the road itself was dark, relieved only by a wartime invention, glinting "cats' eyes" that marked the centre of the road. Mum and Dad had never seen them before. After an interminable time we reached Barneyhill, near Dunbar, Mum's sister's house, a farmhouse belonging to her husband Bobby Hope. Eleanor Hope had gathered there all the cousins and uncles and aunts and grandparents. The house was big and old. Bright candles in silver candlesticks, arranged along the middle of a long, dark, polished table, lit up the cavernous dining room. Twenty of us sat down to dinner served by two maids, Chrissie and Jeanette. The cousins made a great fuss of me and constantly filled up my glass with red wine. A graver personage of whom I was barely aware was my Moderator grandfather, Marshall Lang. One of the topics of the evening concerned the death of the Moderator's elder brother, Cosmo Gordon Lang. Being a recent Archbishop of Canterbury and before that Archbishop of York, Cosmo was clearly a much-revered figure in the family. But I remember mutterings that he had been succeeded at Canterbury by a very good and holy man, Archbishop Temple, who had died some years before. Somehow to me the comparison did not reflect so well on Cosmo. But, of course, it was the Moderator who was my grandfather and for whom I had been taught to sing metrical psalms, not that I ever did in the end. It was he who had baptised me as a comparatively old baby, just before the war when my father was in Britain for a long leave.

PRE-CONSCIOUSNESS:
1938–1942

6 Birth and War

(Population – 2.3 billion; CO2 ppm – 309; Centigrade – +0.4)

My father, Harry Macdonald, was a regular soldier, a captain in the Royal Engineers. In 1935 he was seconded to train Indian troops in the military base at Roorkee, some 200 miles north-east of Delhi. Roorkee was where I was born, on December 8, 1938 at nine-thirty in the evening. My mother, Laurina Lang, an artist by training from the Edinburgh School of Art, was at thirty-seven quite old by the standards of the time. My sister was already five and a half when I came into her world. My father was delighted to have a son and heir. He apparently marched round the house playing his bagpipes. My sister was less than delighted. Why was such a fuss being made of this noisy, annoying little infant just because he was a boy? She was even less delighted, though somewhat intrigued, when my parents held a party in their garden to celebrate my birth. Joan Mary remembered it. It was in the evening, just as the sun was going down and the night was coming on. My father's trainee soldiers all encamped in our garden where they lit numerous fires, round which they sat and cooked their different foods. And they all came up to bless me. I was blessed by Hindus, Muslims, Sikhs, and even by one Buddhist.

Then in May 1939 my father took his long leave in Britain. The family started at Salcombe in Devon and then moved up to Scotland, to East Lothian and Edinburgh where all our closest relatives were living at the time. But in September war broke out. My father was expecting to go straight back to Roorkee, but the War Office had lost his papers. Eventually his soldiers went to North Africa without him. And then later they fought in the battle of El Alamein. My father, though, did finally go back to Roorkee to train more soldiers, while Mum, JM and I were left in North Berwick near my mother's relatives. Of course I do not remember any of this, nor kicking up a fuss when made to wear my Mickey Mouse gasmask, nor being in my pram out in the garden in the midst of one of the coldest and snowiest winters of the century.

But Mum was determined to join Dad in India. Her parents and sisters were totally against it. German U-boats were known to be on the prowl. But at last, despite many a warning, she secured a sailing on *The City of Hong Kong* from Liverpool on September 12. Our sixteen-year-old "nanny" pleaded to come too, but she was one responsibility too many for my mother. Instead, a young Welsh woman travelling out to India in the same ship to join her husband volunteered her services to look after me. Before boarding we stayed a night in a hotel near the Liverpool docks. At some point Joan Mary was woken up by great flashes of light and simultaneous bangs. She thought it was a thunderstorm. But, no. Liverpool was being bombed.

7 Travel – Bombs, Torpedoes, and Tantrums

The ship, however, was not harmed and slid out to sea the next afternoon to join a convoy from Glasgow sailing past the north coast of Ireland. It was not a happy convoy. *The City of Simla* and *The City of Benares* were both sunk, with many lives lost and much terror on *The City of Hong Kong*. After passing Ireland, the convoy split into two. Most of the ships that had survived crossed the Atlantic to Canada and the USA guarded by the Royal Navy. *The City of Hong Kong* turned south and steamed, it seems, on its own towards the Cape of Good Hope at a steady four knots. Why so slow? Because anything faster would have been heard by U-boats.

The voyage for all the passengers was extremely wearisome and stressful. My behaviour was so bad that Mum thought that the young Welsh wife must have been beating me. She was duly relieved of her burden. My behaviour did not improve. I bawled so much at night that the occupants of the cabin next door thumped on the walls till Mum was forced to take refuge with her children in the ship's lounge. There she tried to sleep, telling JM to keep me occupied. Which she did, by chasing me round and round the furniture. But the bawling did not stop, now for a new reason: the ship ran out of vegetables and water. At her wits' end, Mum took me to the ship's doctor. "Now, Mrs. Macdonald," he said, "you may not like this advice, but it is the best I can do. Take him to the bar at midday every day and give him a half pint of beer." My mother was delighted, not only did she have positive medical advice but she also liked the idea of the bar at midday. Joan Mary was not so pleased. She was too young to be allowed into the bar, but thought it unfair that I at a much younger age was allowed. But the advice was indeed good. I quietened down for the rest of the journey including a twenty-four hour landing in Durban. When Dad met the ship in Bombay, the journey had taken more than ten weeks.

8 Vague Memories – Pearl Harbour

Of course I was too young to remember any of that saga, or to have more than the sketchiest memory of the eighteen months in Roorkee before we went to Ranikhet. We did not stay in Roorkee all that time. We spent the hot weather in the hill-station of Mussoorie. It was there that my first memories were formed. Falling off a swing, playing with toys in my evening bath. Being aware that we were staying in a hotel called The Charleville, much beloved, so I found out years later, by anglophile rajahs and maharajahs, disliking Nell, my nannie, whose hair I pulled, so I am told, unmercifully.

I remember Roorkee better. We used to go for picnics in a sandy area where pools of clear water had formed. Joan Mary sailed her beautiful little toy yacht, called *Laurina*, made by my father. Dad had taken part in many sailing ventures before he and my mother left for India. He had rounded the Fastnet Rock in *Ilex* and raced in the first transatlantic yacht race from Newport, Rhode Island to Plymouth. No wonder JM was so keen on dinghies and yachts! More Indian was a religious procession I once saw going past our house. Elephants led the way, their heads and howdahs bedecked with hundreds of bright flowers, and accompanied by loud unusual music and crowds swaying to and fro. More down to earth – I had a passion for collecting bottle tops that lay on the ground outside the kitchen, and JM and I ran races on the grass in the evening sunlight. In the afternoons the heat was oppressive as I lay sweating in my cot shrouded with a mosquito net. One event stood out. The night before my third birthday, news came through on the wireless that Japan had attacked Pearl Harbour. I remember hiding behind the sofa and scribbling on the wall. Apparently my father was rather pleased, because here was a call to action and a situation for which had been trained. And so he was sent to Colombo to enlarge its harbour while Mum, JM, and I went to spend those eighteen months in Ranikhet.

YOUNG BOYHOOD in BRITAIN and Goodbye to the Army, 1946–1948

9 Edinburgh

After our return from India to Scotland, Dad was given his new military posting. He was going to be with Scottish Command in Edinburgh. And so in January 1946 we packed up again to live in a hotel at 19 Palmerston Place. The smoke-blackened buildings of Edinburgh and the constant smell of beer being brewed in the many breweries that then existed were not much to my liking. It also seemed to rain or sleet more than it had in East Lothian. But I found one wonderful pastime. I explored the tramways of Edinburgh. After all, they were pretty much like trains. And so I would board a tram on my own with a tuppence ha'penny child's return ticket to its destination, whether Corstorphine, Fairmilehead, Colinton, or the bottom of Leith Walk. I would sit in a seat at the very front of the top deck and be at the centre of all that I surveyed. In this way I came to have a knowledge of Edinburgh.

Palmerston Place is a quick walk away from the Murrayfield rugby ground. Dad was passionate about rugby. And so we went to watch Scotland play England, Ireland and Wales in unofficial championship matches. They were unofficial, because the rugby clubs were only just recovering from the war; players were neither very fit nor available. Nevertheless, this was my introduction to being a Scot. Without knowing anything about the game, I shouted "Scotland" at the top of my voice as I stood on the terrace, peering out at the game surrounded by people all taller than me also shouting "Scotland". The hero of the season was Tommy Geddes, a name I have never forgotten. He took all the penalty kicks and converted all the tries.

JM and I now had to go to school, she to Rothesay House and I to Angusfield, in Eglinton Crescent. They were both round the corner from Palmerston Place. My teacher was nice but strict, and somewhat different from Mothers Bertram and Columba. There were weekly class orders and I was always bottom. Then I contracted chickenpox, which caused alarm in the hotel, so much so that I spent two weeks boarding at Angusfield where a number of pupils were suffering from the same condition. When I came back into the class, to my amazement my position in it suddenly zoomed to near the top. I accepted the change with some bewilderment, especially as I still found it difficult to spell monster words like "acknowledgment". But I understood grammar, and liked the teacher's comparison of a conjunction to a railway junction. In art classes I drew or painted railway lines vanishing into the distance; the thought of perspective fascinated me. The art teacher, Ruth Monroe, was very encouraging. She and Mum had been to Edinburgh Art School together. In the spring holidays, JM and I paid a visit to our grandparents. They were Mum's parents, the Moderator and his wife. Dad's parents had died before the war. We went on our own by bus to the village of Gifford, which nestles under the Lammermuir hills. Our grandparents had a small house with a veranda that looked over a meadow. Behind it was a wood packed with dark fir trees. I felt out of my depth and at lunch I asked whether they would leave us money when they died. I had the impression that I had said something rather bad.

Our rooms in Palmerston Place were dull and dark, as was Edinburgh itself. One ordinary walk in the countryside outside Corstorphine was notable for being sunlit and for a lark singing somewhere in the blue sky. We also went to the Braids, low hills on the southern edge of Edinburgh. Though I cannot remember sunshine there, at least they were green and did not smell of beer.

Dad was now posted to Halifax and Mum decided to accompany him. And so, for the summer term JM and I had to board in our respective schools. Parting was difficult. A vicious headache took over my brain just before I was due to go, though a couple of pills, a mug of tea and a short sleep cured it. Later I heard that JM had briefly run away from school. Still, it was summer and the days became longer, far longer – so much longer that it was difficult to go to sleep. In the dark of a dormitory I could hear children playing in the gardens of Eglinton Crescent and blackbirds singing loudly. We boys, meanwhile, were forbidden to talk in the dormitory on pain of a beating. Daytime was better. We played very elementary games of cricket. What a complicated game! We watched Merchiston Castle School play Loreto, and went for Sunday walks, two by two, on Ravelston Dykes. On one of these, on a very hot afternoon, we encountered girls from Rothesay House, amongst them being JM. She shouted out to me. I did not know what to do. I was supposed to be walking in a crocodile. I ignored her. We also walked in a crocodile to the great church of St. John's for Sunday Matins. It is a huge, dark, cavernous church. The services were very boring.

10 Winchester

Dad had now yet another new posting. At Barton Stacey near Winchester. And so, when the summer term came to an end, Mum, JM, and I boarded *The Flying Scotsman* bound for London where we would change trains and take another one to Winchester. Great excitement! Another adventure and *The Flying Scotsman*! But *The Flying Scotsman* did not fly; it limped into King's Cross, a disappointing two hours late. Dad met us and we had supper in the station hotel. Then crossing London to Waterloo we boarded the train to Winchester. As the train left the station, Dad exclaimed, "Look! There are The Houses of Parliament!" That was exciting.

Our new hotel was Hyde Abbey House, a large, square seventeenth-century house with creaky stairs and creaky floorboards. It was near a beautiful park with streams of clear water, abounding in minnows and crayfish. It even had a stretch where JM and I could hire a rowing boat to go up and down. But that did not last long. It began to rain, and it rained for most of the rest of the summer. Not that I saw much of it. I began to feel ill at Matins in the cathedral, a service that was no less boring than Matins at St. John's, Edinburgh. I don't think I was bored just because I was going down with measles. Hyde Abbey House, no less than 19 Palmerston Place, disliked housing sick children. I was rushed off to the fever hospital on a hill outside Winchester. Soon I was joined by JM and the hotel cook's small son. We all had measles very badly. When I came out of hospital, the weather had turned completely. We trudged round the town, sheltered in medieval archways from soaking rain, and walked past the famous Winchester College. By that time I had been told, as services children were, that I would go to a boarding public school, probably Cheltenham or

Wellington, schools favoured by the army. "Would you like to go to Winchester College?" my mother asked as we walked past it. The thought horrified me. Its outside walls could have belonged to a grim castle or prison, not a school – and in Winchester it did nothing but rain.

11 Home and Snow

We left Winchester. Dad went back to Halifax and Joan Mary to Rothesay House. Mum and I went to our last hotel, the Golf Hotel in North Berwick. This was because Mum and Dad had bought a house just down Hamilton Road from the hotel and we were due to move in soon. It was part of a grand, posh Edwardian house built for Londoners holidaying by the sea in Scotland. East Lothian had become very desirable for holidays, partly because Arthur Balfour and H.H. Asquith, leaders of the Conservative and Liberal Parties respectively, had homes here. Their families used to take it in turn to entertain the other to Sunday lunch. I had been told this because my Moderator grandfather had been the Balfour's local minister at Whittingehame. As to the house that we had bought, we were to inhabit the servants' end. Dad took great delight in saying that the living room had once been the boiler room; Mum tried to hush him up.

At all events the house was not yet ready and Mum and I stayed in the hotel. I, to my delight, went to school at St. Baldred's, just over the road. It was a little school catering for both boys and girls. I liked it because it was friendly and for the brief two terms that I was there I had good chums. I particularly liked Philip Tranter, the son of Nigel Tranter, the novelist, and James Coates whose family soon emigrated to South Africa. I loved Scottish history: Robert the Bruce and the spider, the Black and Red Douglases, and I hated (in an excited way) Edward I of England, the Hammer of the Scots. At least we won Bannockburn. In fact the school under a Miss Walker was not particularly Scottish. A fair number of English families had been in North Berwick during the war to avoid the bombing raids, and had stayed on.

After the bad summer, October was fine and gently warm. My mother encouraged me to look for cowries on the bright white beaches, or to climb North Berwick Law. Capped by a whale's jaw bone, the conical hill rising 600 feet from almost nowhere looks down upon the craggy islands that lie in a line offshore: Fidra with its odd shape and lighthouse, The Lamb, Craig Leith and some way away the Bass Rock, famous for its myriad gannets, its cliffs white with their guano. James Coates told me in a whisper that North Berwick was once a centre for witches who rode out in their coracles to indulge in séances on the islands. It was easy to believe him, for there were medieval castles too in East Lothian: one in the nearby village of Dirleton and another above the steep, high, red cliffs at Tantallon, overlooking the sea.

Finally Mum and I moved into the house. Our first meal there was memorable. Eaten in the sunny little morning room it was finnan haddock, fresh from the fishmonger and delicious. Mum was very pleased because it was the first meal she had ever cooked for a member of her family. She had only learned to do so by taking cookery lessons at the Red Lion pub in Halifax. It was not much later that she cooked our Christmas dinner for the grandparents as well as for the four of us. I cannot remember being disappointed, nor for that matter were JM or Dad. Dad had come up from Halifax on a seventy-two hours leave.

And so the New Year arrived. It was the prelude to the coldest winter in memory. The snow came down on January 18 (I remember the date vividly) and stayed until early April. We owned a small wooden toboggan that I used to trundle out to the golf course and then hurtle down the short slopes. The nearby beach was full of garden birds pecking away at the seaweed for want of anything better. One afternoon I saw a strange white bird. I did not know what it was until Miss Walker told me that it was probably an albino blackbird. When we went to Gifford in our small pre-war Ford, going very slowly and carefully along skiddy roads, we passed barns and houses dripping with ten-foot icicles. Arriving back home we made sure the car stayed warm enough by wrapping its radiator with rugs, even though it was in a rented garage. There was an extra problem. Coal was rationed. Luckily our living room converted from a boiler room heated up quickly. We lived in it and in the kitchen. Doors were kept tightly shut. I rather liked going to bed in a very cold room where I could snuggle under the blankets clutching my hot water bottle and my teddy bear. It was some time in February that Mum went to visit Dad in Halifax. I was housed with the McCabes, who I liked very much. Matthew was at least three years older than me, but we still played together. I also stayed with Eleanor and Bobby for several days. But it is the nights at Barneyhill that I remember. After the three of us had played uproarious games of Racing Demon in a tiny and bare but warm laundry room, I went up the cold, wide stairs to my bedroom. It had high a ceiling and was very large and cold. It did not help me that Eleanor loved telling ghost stories. But as Eleanor, who was childless, was great fun, I did not really and truly believe them. But she did put *Grimm's Fairy Tales* beside my bed. I read a few pages and did not want to read further. One night I woke up to a tapping on one of the two big windows. They were heavily curtained. Slightly anxious I stepped out of bed and walked quietly towards the window that was being tapped. Slowly drawing back the curtain I saw in the light of a full moon, which shone brightly on the snow, two small owls perched on the window ledge. One was white and the other brown. Amazing! Two different species sitting together. I knew enough to think that this was quite unusual. Some years later when reading Keats' *St. Agnes Eve* I could not help thinking of those two little owls when the poet wrote:

"St. Agnes Eve, Ah bitter chill it was,

The owl for all his feathers was a-cold…"

EDUCATION IN BOARDING SCHOOLS, 1947–1957

12 Stourport-on-Severn

The River Severn was in flood right over its banks. Slabs of ice sailed down its fast-flowing central current. Despite having a house in North Berwick we were yet again in a hotel, Areley House, near the river. And only next term I was going to be a border at Belhaven Hill, a school near Dunbar. I had been prepared well in advance for this change in my life. We had visited it earlier and seen the concrete open-air swimming pool. The headmaster was Brian Simms, who as a young man had been kind to Dad when he had been in a prep school near Nairn thirty years earlier. Because Dad was in the army and liable to be posted to different places, boarding school was the obvious answer to my education. It was normal. Nevertheless, I was apprehensive. This time Dad had been posted from Barton Stacey to Kidderminster. But Areley House was a handsome country hotel near Stourport-on-Severn and exciting new territory. A beautiful garden surrounded the hotel; its lawn was bounded by bushes and trees, places ripe for exploration. And there were lots of small birds. On the first day there I found a blue tit on the drive, frozen solid. I was very sorry for it and gave it a decent burial. Although the sun was now higher in the sky and warmer, winter still had its place. But spring was certainly coming and the days were sunny. We fed the birds from the window ledge of our sunny main room. All sorts came. They seemed to be ravenous. Chaffinches, bullfinches, greenfinches and all manner of tits. Even nuthatches came. I had never seen them in North Berwick. Nor had I seen a Little Owl, one of which I spotted lurking in a thick bush beside the lawn. And when JM and I walked down the country road beside the hotel, we saw a kingfisher perched on a branch over a stream near the stone bridge that carried our road. Areley House may have been yet another hotel, but it was fun. Even so, I did not behave very well. I became fiercely competitive at Racing Demon and Pelmanism and threw tantrums when I lost. "You can't behave like this at Belhaven!" snapped Dad. Dad was not entirely my favourite person. He said I was too old to sit on Mum's lap.

13 Belhaven Hill

I can remember nothing of my first day at Belhaven. I can remember only my first night. My bed in the large dormitory was between those of Robin Trotter, whose name I liked, and Lee Wilson. I could hear the whistles of trains as they rounded the big curve of the main line south. I imagined my parents somewhere down at the terminus of that line. On the Saturday morning, at the end of the first full week, the whole school, forty-eight boys in all, assembled in the senior classroom to hear everyone's marks – A, B, C, or D. I did not know what to expect. But when Mr. Simms had read out some forty lots of marks, he came to "Macdonald". All As except a B in French. There were gasps from the boys. And so I had started, feeling rather embarrassed and proud.

I was somewhat wary of Brian Simms. Yes, he had a twinkle in his eye, but he was old and his tweed suits smelt of tobacco. He taught Latin to the lowest form. I had been introduced to this strange language by my form mistress at St. Baldred's and liked the sense of order in its grammar. This was an advantage. But Mr. Simms had nasty habits if someone made a mistake. "Ah, little kiddy!" he would say as he twisted a poor unfortunate's ear. Or worse, for a worse mistake, one had to eat humble pie. This consisted of kneeling in front of him and burying one's face between his smelly thighs. I suppose this helped me to commit a minimum of such mistakes. In the holidays I described the ear technique to Joan Mary, which made us say laughingly to each other "Ah, little kiddy!" But I never spoke of the smelly thighs. I might have been good at Latin, but French was a different matter. I thought our French book was weedy. It began "*Madame Souris a une maison…*" and was all about mice who could speak French. French was Miss Musson's area. She was the form mistress. I preferred MJ, short for Mr. Martin-Jones. I liked learning about Vasco da Gama and drawing maps of Australia. I forget who taught arithmetic. Perhaps this is because I was caught up in an epidemic of mumps. Mumps disappointed me because I missed the Sports Day, for which Mum and Dad had come up especially from Kidderminster. And it was a good summer, surprisingly. The sick room was bathed in sunshine while I read *Black Beauty* or tried to compete in cherry races starting with the stalk between my teeth and flipping the fruit over into my mouth – something that was difficult to do in the middle of mumps. After that there was not much left of the term except my little garden plot. Everyone had a little plot and took a pride in the flowers they grew. My little plot was sadly neglected. Mumps had got in the way. I was not much bothered; I preferred watching the swallows fly to their nest in and out of the tractor shed which smelt of mown grass.

"Only five days more, only five days more, only five days more till the END of the TERM." So we sang, and the end did finally come. It was a blest summer. Even in North Berwick the temperature hovered between 70 and 75 degrees every day. I met a new cousin when we went one afternoon to Barneyhill; Bill Henderson, a brother of Jean. He had been a parachutist at the battle of Arnhem and loved cricket. "Have you listened to the Test matches against South Africa?" he asked. I hardly knew what he was talking about. "Just follow Edrich and Compton," he said. "They are wonderful batsmen." It still didn't mean much. Dad had our old car in Stourport, but we did manage sometimes to reach Barneyhill, where we picked strawberries and raspberries in the old kitchen garden (and watched the trains go by on the London line). Eleanor gave us eggs and fresh vegetables which, because of food rationing, were in short supply. I longed to swim, but was not allowed, because I had a verucca on the ball of my foot. When that was finally pared off, a bout of polio in North Berwick meant that we could not use the public swimming pool. No matter – the sea was warm enough even if one's teeth chattered incessantly after coming out. One morning JM and I started out on the longest walk I had ever done. From Gullane to North Berwick along the beach, past the golf course at Muirfield, where Henry Cotton had just won the Open (I was beginning to become used to these sports), past the island of Fidra on a very long, wide sandy beach, till we reached the little stream of the Eel Burn as it spread its water over the sand before meeting the sea. That was the frontier of known territory and we had walked at least five miles.

In September I went back to school after visiting my grandparents. I was dressed in an uncomfortable blue Harris Tweed suit and was not looking forward to an ever-darkening winter term. I had been promoted to the fourth form, which was soon combined with the third because one teacher did not appear. It was hard keeping up with the other pupils. I have dim memories of ducking for apples at Halloween, standing in the gloom watching a blazing bonfire and, towards the end of the term, capering on a stage dressed as a jester in the school concert. That took place on my birthday, but I have no recollections of any birthday.

The Christmas holidays arrived. Brian Simms accompanied me to the Caledonian Station in Edinburgh where JM was waiting to travel with me on the train to Wolverhampton. Mum and Dad had rented a small bungalow in a village called Mustow Green. And it was there we celebrated Christmas. Without Father Christmas. Apparently he did not exist. The stockings we received had been bought in Woolworths. They were very flimsy. I did not particularly mind: I had been given a bicycle for a combined Christmas and birthday present. And so for the rest of the holidays, after learning to ride, I raced along the narrow Worcestershire lanes, delighting in the speed and fresh air.

Christmas Day, too, was very cosy with just the four of us, a large Christmas tree, and a blazing fire in the living-room hearth. One evening we were joined by a very jolly major connected somehow to Dad's work. I was not aware of the significance of this at the time, but Dad was leaving the army. That was why the major had come to supper. The reason for this decision was not untypical of the army at the time. After returning from ten years in India, Dad had been told that he would have at least five years in Britain before another posting abroad. But now, after two years, he was being sent to Benghazi in Libya. I loved the idea of all that sunshine and the bright, sandy desert. But Mum was not of that mind at all. She rebelled. She was not going to Benghazi. Years later I learned that there had been a big argument. And Dad did not go to Benghazi, nor did we. I went back to school on my own from Wolverhampton. The train guard was asked to keep an eye on me. And so I spent the next six hours enjoying one of my favourite pastimes, looking out of the window and watching Warrington, Wigan, Preston, and Carlisle all roll by. A friendly man sitting in the same compartment told me which everyday objects were manufactured in each of those towns. Soap in Warrington, apparently, and rubber tyres in Wigan. Arriving back in Edinburgh I spent the night at Aunt Amy's house in Morningside before going on to Belhaven. Aunt Amy was two years older than Dad. She and Mum did not get on.

Life was beginning to move faster. A new teacher came to Belhaven with his American wife. He was stout and wore a tweed suit. He did so even when refereeing our junior soccer games. In one of these I was kicked in the balls, which was extremely painful. His wife tended to my injury, which I appreciated. Soon after, the two of them disappeared, never to be seen again. Once more the third and fourth forms were amalgamated. But years later I recognised this man as the headmaster of an unusual and academically successful private preparatory school, which he had bought when he disappeared from Belhaven.

14 Civvy Street

We spent the Easter holidays in North Berwick. I was aware
of it being a difficult time. Dad was trying to find a job in
Scotland, one that paid well enough to keep his children in
private education. But it was not easy, and he had to settle
for one in Nottingham, at the Ministry of Agriculture and
Fisheries. In those days the services paid officers enough for
private boarding schools because postings were so varied,
whether they were in Libya, Germany or Hong Kong.
But Dad lost that emolument, and thereafter money was
always short. Dad's morale was dented; he had liked being
a soldier and had been looking forward to promotion. For
Nottingham, however, I developed a liking, even before I
stayed there. That was because of cricket. Compton and
Edrich were still in the English cricket team. The First Test
match was played in Nottingham, at Trent Bridge, and
the series was about the Ashes. Mum sent me newspaper
articles: the great Bradman scored 135 and so did his vice-
captain, Hassett, while for England Compton scored 185 in
the second innings. Though England lost, I was enthused.
Back in East Lothian, Eleanor and Bobby, who looked
after me on the few Sundays that I was allowed out from
school, were very keen on cricket, particularly the Third Test
match in which Compton scored 145 before rain put an
end to the game. Eleanor knew all about it. It was played in
Manchester, and Eleanor took the *Manchester Guardian*. The
climax of the season was going to be in Edinburgh. Yes, the
Fifth Test was played at the Oval in London, but England
was skittled out by the Australian fast bowlers, Lindwall and
Millar. Much more important for me was the game at the
end of the season against Scotland. I was actually going to
see Bradman playing! I was very excited. I could not sleep

the night before the game. But… when I finally got up, I looked out of the window, and saw a leaden sky… and rain. I was disappointed to the core. Since then I have always guarded against too much excited anticipation, a defensive state of mind I have christened "Doing a Don Bradman". In the end we did see him bat, on a curtailed second day. I took away an image of him almost dancing when he hit the ball, so nimble was he on his feet. But Bradman was now forty years old and had played his last Test match.

Britain, however, was slowly looking up. And I was aware of this. There was a Festival of Britain in 1948, held mostly in London, but celebrated in the press. And the 1948 Olympic Games, the first after the war, were held at Wembley. A noticeable star was Fanny Blankers-Koen, a Dutch woman who flew along in the shorter races, her blonde ponytail streaming out behind her. Almost as celebrated was the dark-haired British sprinter who always came second, Maureen Gardner.

I was becoming more aware of Britain as a whole, partly because we spent at least part of the next four school holidays in Nottingham. In the early days we lived in a small flat at the top of 486 Mansfield Road, a main road leading north out of the city. The flat was so small that JM and I shared a box room for our bedroom. A curtain divided the two sides in a decorous fashion. We spent Christmas there, enlivened for me, at least, by an interesting cricket series in South Africa. But it was a very small flat indeed and I often left it to wander around Nottingham on my own. I walked for miles in modern pre-war housing estates and some grimy-looking slums, as well as in more welcoming parks and avenues. I came to know the city so well that I might even now know my way around, despite the inevitable changes. As a family we also came to know the area outside the city. Dad's job included inspecting camps for people displaced after the war. We used to go and have lunch in them, not that I personally liked the lunches; too often the meat consisted of globby fat. But I enjoyed it when we motored along Roman roads like Watling Street, Erskine Street, and The Fosse Way. Cars were not as wonderful as trains but I could still look out through the window. And so I came to know the deep-soiled expanses of Lincolnshire and the rocky hills around Buxton. Leicester was the town with the most television masts.

In Towcester lived a wonderfully kind and genial bachelor, a great-uncle on Mum's side of the family called Norman Lang. Uncle Norman was the first person of his generation to whom I was drawn. Like his brother Cosmo he too was a bishop, a suffragan of Peterborough whom Mum had never met before. He lived in a big house with a housekeeper who baked delicious cakes topped with creamy icing. We loved going there, not just for the tea, but because Uncle Norman was a good raconteur with a lively sense of humour. He adored walking and climbing in the Scottish Highlands, and when I told him about the Himalayas he listened with rapt attention and told me that I "must walk and climb in the Highlands of Scotland".

After two holidays in No. 486 we rented a flat in 9 Corporation Oaks. This was something of a relief. The landlord of No. 486 who lived below us had been constantly complaining about my "hobnailed boots", as he called my youthful steps. No. 9 was much larger, rather ramshackle, but very pleasant. We lived there in the summer and then at Christmas. Food rationing was still in force, and indeed even more straitened. One day Mum dished up some very strange meat. She asked us to guess what it was. We tried everything but we did not get close to the right answer. "It's whale meat!" she announced rather triumphantly. She never served it again. It was from there that we drove out into the countryside to Newstead Abbey, once the home of Lord Byron. At that time it was run down and deserted but it had an attractive lake by which we sometimes picnicked. Trees lined one shore and it was there that I learnt to climb. "Always have one foot and one hand firmly based!" said my military father. We spent one whole Saturday watching the New Zealand cricket team playing Nottinghamshire. It was not a Test match and perhaps a bit dull. But I did spend two more days watching on my own. I was hooked.

Then, at last, Dad was offered a job in Edinburgh. We left Corporation Oaks just after New Year's Day in 1950 and motored up the A1 in our old pre-war Ford, stopping at Scotch Corner for the night in a very big red-brick hotel. Then on to Otterburn for lunch, where Mum's elder sister, Hannah and her husband, Bill, owned and ran the Otterburn Tower Hotel, much frequented by gunners practising their skills on the range at Redesdale up towards the Scottish border. Finally we crossed over the rolling border hills at Carter Bar, into Scotland. We were home.

15 East Lothian

While we lived in Nottingham, I was going slowly up the school at Belhaven. Brian Simms retired and his position was taken over by the young enthusiastic number two, Willie Caldwell. The atmosphere of the school immediately became lighter. The dress regulations were relaxed; Harris Tweed suits were not needed. There was a palpable feeling of modernity. Nevertheless, it was still a boarding school and we were allowed to go home only for occasional Sundays.

Life was not easy for a number of my contemporaries. I was lucky. Although I was small and early on, at least, boasted of having lived in India, I was never really bullied, though one or two boys were. At the time I put that down to a contrived use of swear words. But it was more because I was seen as clever (not that that necessarily warded off the bullies), but despite my size I was good at games and played for all the first teams before I was eleven, much encouraged by Colin Mason, the brother of James the Hollywood actor (who at that time Colin loathed). With that boost to my confidence, I truly enjoyed Belhaven. It was (and is) a good-looking school. The large Adam-style house built of local stone was in the middle of attractive grounds. There were playing fields, of course, but also two grass tennis courts, a squash court, a large, walled kitchen garden full of soft, summer fruits, apples and vegetables, an open-air swimming pool, and all round its perimeter there were trees and bushes where many species of small birds nested. That was a delight for me; in my last summer term, I drew a map of the grounds and marked in more than 300 nests, which friends and I had discovered, our favourite being a nest of blackcaps, which at the time were rare in Scotland. We were also taken on hikes and bird-watching expeditions outside the school, either through the round-bottomed glens running up to the heathery Lammermuirs or to the headland beyond the estuary of the North Tyne where a large colony of terns nested in the summer; or, best of all, to Fast Castle set on its rugged sea cliffs where there was supposed to be a pair of peregrine falcons. We never saw them, but we did see ravens and rock pigeons. And in my last two summer terms I was allowed to play golf with Peter Jamieson and Robin Grant on the open golf course that stretched out over a headland towards the wide, shimmering sands of Belhaven Bay.

I liked being outside in the fresh air. My father who played the piano as well as bagpipes suggested lightly that I should take music lessons like so many of my friends, but I could see hours of practising ahead of me and did not like the idea. I would have much preferred to draw and paint. Unfortunately, I once painted a red tulip black and Miss Musson reprimanded me roundly: "You stupid boy! You can't do that sort of thing!" And so, unwillingly, I was dropped from art and took up Greek, with lifelong consequences. (Later I was found to be colour blind, a fate encountered by 8 per cent of male humans.) Belhaven, however, provided many opportunities for activities indoors, especially in the winter. Drama was taken seriously and those who could (and even those who couldn't) were taught to sing properly. Debating was encouraged. Near the end of my time the Labour prime minister, Clement Attlee, called a General Election, which the Conservatives won. And so, we held an election in the school just before the real election. The Tory candidate was Michael Clark-Hutchinson, the son of a would-be Tory MP in Edinburgh. At that time at least, he was as determinedly jingoistic and parochial as his father. And so I decided, partly for that reason, to be the Labour candidate even though I hoped that the Tories would win the real election. My agent was Magnus Linklater, who at only nine years of age was much more knowledgeable about politics than me. The two of us were very happy to secure 35 per cent of the poll, in a school that was fundamentally Conservative. Years later Magnus was a very respected political journalist.

But now it was time to move on. Not to Wellington College nor to Cheltenham. They were "army" schools and Dad was no longer in the army. I had hoped to go to Marlborough, the destination of some friends and where, according to MJ, Dartford Warblers were to be found in the Savernake Forest. I liked too the thought that the South of England would be warmer than Scotland. My destination, however, was to be Trinity College, Glenalmond, situated on the edge of the Scottish Highlands. Mum and Dad wanted me to be in Scotland. Edinburgh Academy, where Dad had been during the First World War, was a possibility, especially because being a day school it was cheaper. But I hated the idea of dark, black Edinburgh, and so Glenalmond was chosen. But that depended on me winning a scholarship. Which I did, but only by the narrowest of margins. And so, it was a sad goodbye not just to friends, but also to Willie Caldwell, Keith Martin-Jones, Colin Mason, and Miss Musson, whose Christian name I don't think any one of us ever found out.

16 Trinity College, Glenalmond

I had never seen Glenalmond before taking the scholarship, but I did in the summer holidays between leaving Belhaven and going there. I was a guest of the Innes twins, Malcolm and James, who left Belhaven at the same time as me. They lived in a large, dark house beside the River Almond. It was dark because for much of the time that I was there it was raining. This had one advantage: the river was in spate. Sea trout were coming up. I liked the idea of fishing, and so the twins taught me. Because of the spate, we fished with a worm. On my second cast there was a mighty yank on my rod. I was so surprised that I yanked too. The fish, undoubtedly a big one, got away... On the one dry afternoon the three of us took part in a cricket match at Glenalmond. The only detail that I remember was meeting

Ralph Barlow, the headmaster. He seemed pleased to see me, which helped me cope with my apprehensions at going to a new school. Glenalmond is a very handsome school, an Oxbridge college as it were, set in dignified isolation halfway between Perth and Crieff. A Victorian gatehouse stands at the head of a long avenue which descends past cricket fields and rugby pitches before turning right beside tall Wellingtonias, finally to face the school full on. William Gladstone founded it in 1847 as an Episcopalian school. Its chapel was designed by the distinguished High Victorian architect Sir Ninian Comper. Since a chapel service was compulsory twice a day, we came to know it well. I was deemed fit to sing as a treble in the choir. The highlight was to be a performance of Handel's Messiah in the Perth town hall. I was enormously impressed by this mighty and, to me, complicated work. But I hated, with a deep hatred, rehearsals where the trebles were blamed for everything that went wrong. And so, by my second term I made sure that my voice was breaking.

This was not the only occasion on which I tested the system. I was a scholar but had not been put into the scholarship year. It was quite clear that I had not performed even near my best in the exam, despite coming second in advanced mathematics and Greek. The result was that, along with Andrew Primrose who was in the same situation, I became very pushy: "We ought to be with the scholars!" Mum and Dad supported me and Andrew and I were promoted the following term. The consequence was that we had to sit our O levels after two terms instead of three and be given special tuition on Chaucer, his Pardoner's and Nun's Priest's Tales. The tuition was given by the talented wife of the Head of English. Andrew and I loved Chaucer's language, the delightful story of Chauntecleer, Pertelote and Renard the Fox and the Pardoner's witty homily about avarice. Some subjects we had to drop completely: general science and additional mathematics, and so by the end of the summer I passed only the seven subjects that I took, and never had the chance to become scientifically literate. I did not mind too much at the time, but such ignorance has been a handicap. I was even stymied in history, a subject which I liked. But in the exam I wrote only three essays out of five and was relieved to pass by one mark. But this meant I was advised not to take the subject at A level but instead be content with Ancient History along with Latin and Greek (with English Literature thrown in).

And so my first term at Glenalmond was at best a qualified success. I was very relieved in my second term to have left the new boys' holding house outside the main grounds of the school. I did not like the housemaster who was more interested in consolidating his social position with the landed gentry of Perthshire than being amicable to most of his charges. Now in the main school buildings I had a new housemaster and a reshuffle of friends. The housemaster, Dot Hayes, was new to his house too – a difficult time for someone in that position, especially as his predecessor, "Daudet" Hayward, was reluctant to relinquish control; he used to invite boys in the middle of the house to bridge lessons in his room made particularly attractive by a roaring fire and coffee with biscuits. I came to know him well in my second term because a namesake of mine, "Sanna" Macdonald, and I used to rise very early to help Daudet mark out tracks for the athletics, which took place in the second half of the term. The spring that year was dry and sunny and we loved the scent of the grass and the pine trees and the clear view of the hills that rose on the other side of the valley.

In the summer term, early in June, there was a special three-day holiday to celebrate the Coronation of Queen Elizabeth II. We all went home. Though the Coronation day was wet and cold, it did feel special. There was huge excitement about the new Elizabethan Age with Winston Churchill to the fore. I had read his *The Gathering Storm* and *Their Finest Hour* and was an enthusiastic patriot. The enthusiasm became even greater when the news came out on the Coronation day itself that Hillary and Tensing achieved the first ascent of Mount Everest. For me it was a sort of homecoming and back to the Himalayas.

At the beginning of my second year I had a new form master who in time I came to know well. He was the Head of the Classics department, Charlie Millar. He was another housemaster and popular, though slightly feared, amongst his charges. He tapped into my rudimentary interest in Roman archaeology, which I had developed in Nottingham. He had become a friend of the archaeologist, Sir Ian Richmond, when the latter excavated a Roman camp at Fendoch, further up the Almond valley from the school. The camp had housed an auxiliary unit and guarded the Sma' Glen, the steep and narrow defile into the Highlands out of which the River Almond flows. It was a link in a chain of defences set up by the Roman commander, Agricola, when he was trying to pacify the Caledonian highlanders at the end of the first century AD. Richmond was an expert in this field and with Charlie, I went to Inchtuthil to visit his most famous excavation, at the legionary camp guarding the similar but more important valley of the River Tay. I spent a day there, one summer holidays, getting a taste of archaeology at a time when the impressive sewers of the hospital unit had just been opened up and a huge cache of Roman nails in mint condition had been discovered. On another occasion in the spring holidays a group of us went with Charlie for a tour of Hadrian's Wall. He stayed at The George Hotel, Chollerford while the four of us camped in pup tents beside the River Tyne. In the evening we all had dinner in the hotel and afterwards played Slippery Anne, a card game that Charlie clearly loved. It was a beautiful spring. Following the wall as it wound up and around on its craggy ridges, we could hear the haunting, wavering call of the curlews in the rough ground to the north, where the white bob-tails of rabbits seemed to be everywhere.

It was at about this time that Dad and Mum moved house from North Berwick to Inveresk, a rather grand village to the east of Edinburgh, with some large eighteenth-century houses lying back from its main street. It sits on a bluff above the River Esk; Agricola had made it the meeting place of his two military roads, one running up from the west of Britain and one up the east coast before veering westwards to make the meeting. Professor Richmond had been busy here too. There had been a Roman camp at the top of the bluff where the large kirk now stands. The story goes that Richmond pleaded with two sextons intent on their task for an afternoon burial. "Please, would it be possible," he asked, "to dig two feet deeper so that I can confirm the position of the corner of the commander's praetorium?" He was an expert on Roman military camps. The sextons dug the two extra feet, and the corner was duly confirmed.

The move of homes was done to enable Dad to commute more quickly to his work in Leith and JM too, for her work in the Edinburgh Royal Infirmary as secretary to the eminent physician, Dr Derek Dunlop. I did not much like it. I was just beginning in North Berwick to be aware of girls, and felt adrift in Inveresk. I missed the North Berwick golf course with its view of islands and expanses of beach. I missed the East Lothian light. The light in Inveresk was more sombre. And I did not know enough about architecture to appreciate those big houses. Nevertheless, it did mean that I became more involved in Edinburgh's cultural activities, especially when the newly founded Edinburgh Festival was in progress. We went to the famous Tattoo on the castle esplanade, to concerts in the Usher Hall, to exhibitions of the Scottish Colourists, of Henry Moore and Epstein, and browsed in the bookshops. There was much to ponder in the outside world, both at home and at school. My thrill at the British invasion of the Suez Canal turned to puzzlement when Charlie Millar thought it was a disgraceful act.

Why did he think that? (I was sure that my father did not.) However, our views agreed over the Hungarian uprising, which had all the more resonance when Bela de Csillery, the famous violinist, came to be a teacher at Glenalmond. His first pupil, who had a great regard for him, was Sanna Macdonald.

17 Mountains

I now began to climb mountains. A big one near Glenalmond was Ben Chonzie on the west side of the Sma' Glen. I went up it once as a part of a Combined Cadet Force field day. I was supposed to be leading several platoons over the mountain to "attack" a force situated in the valley below. Somehow the attack came to nothing. I can't remember ever seeing the defending force. But I do remember suddenly finding that I had lost a Very pistol that I was carrying. I had to report the matter to Sergeant-

Major Cheseborough. "Look here, laddie!" he said with some asperity. "I have to account for every single item in my charge. This is a serious matter! The Scottish Republican Army is gaining recruits, fast! Go and find it, laddie!" Oh dear, I thought. This looks more serious than I imagined. After all, the pistol was made in 1917. Nevertheless I decided that I had better make some effort to find it. So, up Ben Chonzie I trudged once again one sunny Sunday afternoon. (It is a very dull, round mountain covered with deep heather and peat hags.) But I always enjoyed being out on these hills, especially as on this occasion I spotted some way off a golden eagle circling in the sky. There was also a large herd of red deer grazing in and out of the peat hags near the top. They started to scatter when they caught wind of my presence. Jumping down time and again from the heather into the runnels of peat I followed them. On one jump, suddenly, a tiny fawn rose to its feet and tottered away. And there, glinting in the impress left by its body in the black, shiny peat, was the pistol. I felt like Aeneas spotting the Golden Bough.

Every Saturday in the summer term boys were let loose in the countryside at midday and not allowed back till six o'clock. More senior boys were free to take a tent and stay out till Sunday evening. Since I played cricket for the First XI, I took part in only one of these expeditions. On this occasion two parties set out in two cars, each driven by a teacher. Our car, with the large and sprightly Jim Greenwood (soon to be Scotland's rugby captain) at the wheel, went to Glenmore Lodge near Aviemore, the other to Braemar. In between lay the high, rounded, heather-clad Cairngorm Mountains split in two by the dark pass of the Lairig Ghru. Here the two parties met to exchange car keys and then pass on. We had first climbed Ben MacDhui in freezing rain. And then walking rapidly towards Braemar we followed such a good path down the long upper reaches of the River Dee that our speed averaged five miles an hour.

I walked and climbed mostly during the summer holidays, along the rugged west coast opposite the Isle of Skye, from Loch Nevis to Loch Maree. The southernmost part, between Loch Nevis and Loch Hourn is known as the Rough Bounds. And rough it is, yet incredibly beautiful. Even now, you can reach it only on foot or by boat. I never saw any other climbers or walkers there. It was wonderfully lonely. I first went with two school friends, Dolly Roberts and Max Reid. We took the train to Glenfinnan, which lies at the head of Loch Shiel where Bonnie Prince Charlie raised his standard. Then after passing under the famously picturesque viaduct our route took us up the steep, pathless glen towards Loch Arkaig. Then turning west through rocky Glendessary, we looked down on the Loch of Heaven, a name sometimes given to the fjord-like Loch Nevis. We could see quite clearly down to the loch below where a seal was stalking a salmon, their forms dark against the pure white sand at the bottom of the water. There is a nipple-shaped mountain, Sgùrr na Cìche, in this remotest of regions. We camped for two nights in an abandoned croft called The Sourlies. It is now a bothy for Munro-bagging climbers. We weren't bagging any mountains but we crossed the valley sinking deep into the wide marsh to climb this beautiful hill, from which we could see the wild and craggy landscapes of the Rough Bounds. And that was the sort of way it was. The weather was seldom good. But the mountains had beautiful shapes. Ben Aden was a rock-bound plug, an impregnable fortress, and the great corrie-gouged mountain of Ladhar Bheinn rose up like a monster lion out of Loch Hourn, the Loch of Hell. It was just so wild and wonderful. Other mountains we climbed nearby on another expedition were The Saddle and the Five Sisters of Kintail, graceful ladies that stand tall above Loch Duich. There was also Ben Sgriol, with its steep, long scree sliding down its southern side into Loch Hourn.

The most memorable of these trips was to Loch Torridon. Here the weather was glorious and the red sandstone mountains, topped by white quartz, glowed in the sunshine, such a contrast to the black Rough Bounds. From Ben Eighe we could see the Cairngorms some hundred miles to the east. Liathach gave us the most excitement as we picked our way along the narrowest of tracks at the top, with a precipice on one side and the steepest of grassy slopes on the other. The gentlest of these Torridonian sandstone mountains is Ben Alligin, which we climbed to gain a view of the Cuillins on Skye, pointed but shadowy shapes in the afternoon heat haze. That expedition ended with a huge haul of small trout, often caught three to a line in the fast-flowing river between Lochan Fada and Loch Maree. They behaved more like the mackerel that the postman caught when he gave us a lift across Loch Hourn from the scallop-rich Barrisdale Bay to the little village of Arnisdale beneath Ben Sgriol.

These expeditions tended to last ten days to a fortnight with little chance of staying in touch with my parents. But we had a safe base, if necessary, at Druidaig on the south side of Loch Duich, where Ian Macrae and his two sisters, Iona and Onie, lived. They were second cousins to Mum and delightfully hospitable and enthusiastic, seldom rising from their beds before midday, and never turning in before the next day's dawn. Druidaig was a house frequented by the well-known Scottish painter, Joseph Farquharson, also related to Mum. Most of his canvases of sheep in snow were, however, painted on the east side of Scotland at his Aberdeenshire estate in Finzean.

18 Passing Exams

My time at Glenalmond was coming to an end. There were A levels to be passed and academic work to be done. I was fairly proficient in Latin and Greek, preferring the content of what we studied to the minutiae of language. Nevertheless the minutiae had to be mastered. I liked Ancient History, particularly the worlds of the Minoans and the Mycenaeans, of Herodotus and Thucydides. But Greek and Latin poetry was beginning to appeal, and not just the fantasies, humour, and lampooning in which Aristophanes indulged. Allan Massie was a great help when we studied English together. We read Jane Austen's *Emma* when we were fifteen, far too young for my unsophisticated mind. Allan was different. He liked *Emma*; I pretended to, in order to keep up with him, and in so doing gained some understanding. Allan was very interested in cricket and the two of us became avid followers of the Ashes tour of 1954/5, to the extent that we wrote a letter to the *Scottish Daily Express* complaining about the coverage written by the retired Aussie cricketer, Sidney Barnes. The letter was published under the pseudonyms of Bunbury and MacNab. Allan was a great admirer of Marilyn Monroe, I of Audrey Hepburn. We wrote away for signed photographs and to our amazement received them by return of post.

The school now entered us for scholarships at Oxford and Cambridge. My father was apprehensive. He could not pay for me unless I won a scholarship, and even then he might not afford the outlay. Scots at that time did not qualify for grants at English universities, and so I might have to go to Edinburgh University. For the moment that was where things were left. In the meantime, down we went to London on the night train, on my birthday, a Saturday in December, seven of us in all. Having a Sunday to kill we went to the National Gallery, where I recognised some of the paintings. Then there was a sexy film in Soho, of Brigitte Bardot doing a striptease. Finally Paddington Station and the train to Oxford for those of us not going to Cambridge. Checking in at the porters' lodge at Oriel College, I was directed to a room in an old whitewashed and beamed building above rooms belonging to Professor Hugh Trevor-Roper. Ah! I thought to myself. He was one of the first pupils at Belhaven. A lucky sign? I had even read his book, *The Last Days of Hitler.*

It was all very strange. We sat down to do our first paper in the dining hall where we had had breakfast. There must have been fifty of us, taking exams in different subjects. Very soon I felt extremely sick. I had to go out to throw up. But there was no invigilator. What was I to do? I went out, was very sick, and returned. Somehow my mind was clear, but within the next two hours I was sick again. But I finished the paper, possibly quite well. In the afternoon there was another three-hour paper. Again I was sick, and this continued for another twenty-four hours. But I survived, felt lucky that one of the questions required a translation from *The Birds* of Aristophanes, a passage that I knew. Another good sign? The last paper was Latin translation. It was rather hard, and it was difficult to concentrate because the London train left Oxford soon after the end of the exam. But I caught it and was able to meet up with my friends who had gone for their examinations in Cambridge. We had a celebratory supper in Soho, paid for by Hamish Macpherson's parents.

I heard nothing from Oriel. Mum and Dad waited. I waited. And waited. It was Christmas Eve, and I had given up. I went to Murrayfield with friends to watch a Scottish rugby trial. Jim Greenwood was playing. We were joined by Angus MacIntyre, the Glenalmond chaplain. "Well done, Jock! Congratulations!"

"What do you mean, Sir?"

"Have you not seen *The Scotsman*? You've won a Major Scholarship to Oriel!"

"No-o-o! Have I really?"

"Of course! Well done!" And so it was. But was I going to be able to take it up? That was the next question.

19 Intermission

Oriel wanted me to go up before National Service, which, in their opinion would get in the way of academic achievements. My father was not too happy, but he gave way. And so it was decided I would see out the academic year at Glenalmond, play cricket for the third year running with the first eleven, and fill in as a teacher. Glenalmond agreed to put up the value of my scholarship there by £30. But how was my scholarship at Oriel to be enhanced?

Living near Glenalmond was a certain Sir Alexander Cross. He had once been an intimidating executive at J & P Coats, so the story went. Then he had a car accident. He was badly hurt, particularly around his head. And that changed his character. He became a delightful philanthropist and with his considerable fortune founded the Cross Trust to help young Scots widen their horizons. I knew him because he often visited Glenalmond and, indeed, became a member of the Glenalmond Council. With his shock of white hair and bouncy demeanour he was easy to recognise. He was Sir Sandy to everyone. But what fascinated us boys was the hole in his forehead, with a membrane in it that expanded and contracted as he spoke. We found it difficult not to stare at it. He used to invite groups of us out to lunch and regale us with steak and kidney pie washed down with sparkling Moselle. It was hard not to come back to school feeling tipsy. But it was Sir Sandy who made sure that I went to Oxford. Indeed, he made sure that for four years I was rather well off with a grant of £300 per year on top of my £100 scholarship. My father was hugely relieved.

In the interval between school and university, I was invited up to Finzean to go to the Aboyne balls. The Finzean estate had for many years belonged to a significant sept of the Farquharson clan. But an Archie Farquharson in the eighteenth century had led a riotous life and suffered the misfortune of crossing the local witch, who cursed him with a curse that prevented any male Farquharson directly inheriting the estate. In the twentieth century Sir Joseph Farquharson inherited it, indirectly. He was an artist of great talent who after travelling and painting abroad settled down in Finzean, painting there and also around Loch Duich. In his sixties he decided that he ought to marry. And this he did with his neighbour's daughter, who at the time was in her twenties. Unfortunately, the day after the wedding – much to the disapproval, one supposes, of his bride – he joined a party shooting pheasants. He came back less of a man, which pleased his wife even less. But he was a wonderful artist. He painted "*en plein air*" which was in vogue at the time, but he took it to an extreme: in the depths of winter he painted sheep in snow. For this he earned the nickname Frozen Mutton Farquharson, a name that after his wedding day had a double significance. When he died without an heir (like all Finzean lairds), the estate passed to a distant cousin, who was a bachelor. Then in turn it passed to my uncle, William Marshall Farquharson Lang, commonly known as Farkie; he had once been the colonial civil servant in the Sudan responsible for education. He returned finally to Scotland in 1955 and in a sense announced his arrival to the other lairds in the region by arranging a party at the Aboyne balls for his eighteen-year-old daughter, my cousin Alison.

Alison had been educated in England. She had been brought up there by her aunts while her parents were away, particularly during the Second World War. And so up to Aboyne came two of her school friends, Barbara Moir and Jenny Keir-Cross. Jenny earlier that summer had been presented to the Queen, and thus had "come out". Going to Highland balls was a natural climax for young women who had just "come out". Barbara was a good golfer and was due to represent the Scottish girls against the French girls on my old golf course at North Berwick.

My cousin David, the elder brother of Bill, Jean and Tony, and now a housemaster at St. Bee's was drafted in to be an avuncular male at the party. Also coming was my school and hill-walking chum, James Wright. David collected me in his old pre-war black Austin and together we drove on a hot, sunny, early September day over the Cairn O'Mount, one of the highest and prettiest of the Highland passes. At the top we stopped to breathe in the fresh scent of heather and honey. Then we dropped down into the Feugh Valley and the hamlet of Finzean. The Feugh is the first of the Highland Glens in those parts and enjoys its own micro-climate, defended by a line of low hills – in the east from fair-weather fog rolling in from the North Sea, and in the west from Atlantic rain by the mass of Lochnagar. Finzean too has its hills, Clach-na-Ben where Satan took a bite out of the top of the hill and spat it out on the side, with results that are clear to see, and Peter Hill, a round heather-clad mountain, its stillness broken only by the "Go back, go back" of startled red grouse. The hills to the north of the valley are lower and less noticeable but up the valley from Finzean there are remains of the old Caledonian forest, its Scots pines inhabited by capercaillie, the largest British bird, now close to extinction. Farkie and his predecessor had worked hard to make the estate productive. Most of its trees had been cut down for the war effort and new trees had to be planted. The bottom of the valley provides good fodder for cattle and is also suited to growing barley and oats. Sheep pasture in the hills as they did in Frozen Mutton's day. It was, and still is, an idyllic land. On and off over the years my family and I have visited Finzean. I once expressed a wish to be buried there.

Alison and Angus and their three children have always been enormously hospitable. In 1957, however, Farkie and his family were perforce living in nearby Banchory. Violet, the widow of Frozen Mutton, was still living in Finzean House, looked after by her butler. Some years earlier the west wing of the house had caught fire and been destroyed. Farkie oversaw its reconstruction, which was difficult for both him and Violet, particularly just after the war when materials and labour were scarce. Every Sunday he used to visit her at teatime when she said little except "Farquharson! I knae' you wish that I were deid". It wasn't till fourteen years later that the poor woman did die: too late for Farkie and my aunt Sheila to live in the house. That fell to Alison and her gentle husband, Angus.

Dancing the night through at the Aboyne balls, three nights out of four, was a gruelling experience. Alcohol and huge meals did not make it easier. But it was the new experience of living in a house with girls that I fancied which made it even more difficult. Jenny was the one. I liked Barbara; I admired her golf. Indeed I caddied for her when later she played against her French counterpart. But Jenny was the more stylish. She was a dark brunette with blue eyes, and helped me put my sporran together when it broke. Dancing with her provoked unwanted reactions. She became my link with Oxford and London.

OXFORD UNIVERSITY, 1957–1961

20 First Loves and Studies

A month after Finzean I was on board the night train to London. I was very excited. Not only was I on the threshold of a new life, but I had arranged to meet Jenny outside the Royal Academy of Music, where she was on a two-year course for helping young people who had hearing and speech impediments. I made sure that I was early, but I was disappointed when it was her mother who finally met me. Jenny was not well. Would I mind coming to their house in Halsey Street? And so I spent half the day with Jenny in her room listening to records of *West Side Story* and *My Fair Lady*. On the train up to Oxford, my only thoughts were of her. And so, over the next six months I took the train up to London as often as was possible. We went to theatres and films: *The Entertainer, Lysistrata,* a who-dunnit, and we ate in a cosy little restaurant off Sloane Square. But in the end she had had enough of this shy and unsophisticated Scot, and one early summer's evening looking at her most glamorous she gently thought that we had better end it.

Thoughts of Jenny certainly coloured my first year at Oxford. But there was a lot to be engaged in. I played hockey for the college. I had not played the game since I was thirteen, and so I was put on the left wing and became known as The Flying Scot, becoming more proficient with my stick at the same time. There were also games of squash in the evenings and listening to classical music with Ken Bartlett, who knew my state of mind. Ken was a fellow classicist but two years older because he had done his National Service in some style, it seemed, in Singapore. But in my year, unlike most other National Service men who had been to a public school, Ken had no side. He was a "very parfit gentle knight".

I enjoyed my studies for classical mods and liked my tutor, Reggie Burton. He was very affable, but had the reputation of not pushing his students very hard. He certainly did not push me. The most important teaching he did was to encourage me to study the epinician poet Pindar. Pindar was thought to be a very difficult poet to translate. And so he was a challenge. But Reggie never encouraged me to write any essays, do any reading outside the set books, or do much more than one piece of translation each week "in my own time". Apart from conventional academic and sporting activities, my life had its ups and downs. I was very much up in my second year when I was with Belinda Sweeting, a lovely girl who came from Wakefield.

Like so many girls at that time, she worked as a secretary, at Headington High School in Oxford. We were mutually attracted. I loved listening to her describing her life in Yorkshire. There was a lilt in her voice. She was pretty and much admired. We saw each other often of an evening in the summer term. The classical examination, the marathon Honour Moderations, fourteen three-hour papers in all, were well and truly over, and the prospect of sitting Finals seemed far off. We used to go punting on the Cherwell, or spend the evening in the comfortable flat that she shared with a friend. If the friend was away, we would happily make love – even if not completely; in those days contraception was not fully understood, or certainly not by us. We went to the Oriel Commemoration Ball, and she came up to Edinburgh with her mother for the Edinburgh Festival, where the two of us watched the Royal Swedish Opera Company put on *Rigoletto*.

Ken and I both got Seconds in Honour Mods, with which we were somewhat disappointed. I had an excuse, I thought. Three weeks before the exam Ken and I had played a late night game of squash followed by a few pints of beer. I, then, in the early hours of the morning, woke up with a terrible pain in my stomach. I was rushed off to hospital, told that I had appendicitis, and received the impression that I was of some interest to medical students because the condition was possibly exacerbated by the beer I had drunk. I was in the Radcliffe for a week. One day I was asked to help with another patient. He was an eighty-year-old blind Russian and spoke no English. Somehow the nurses found out that he spoke Latin. And so I was called in to be an interpreter. I have no idea how effective I was, but I did find out that he was a relative of Boris Pasternak. "You must read *Dr Zhivago,*" was what I gleaned from his acquaintance. So read him I did in the long summer vacation. It is indeed a wonderful, strange book that I have now read three times, each time appreciating it more.

Ken and I then went on to read Greats. That third year started badly for me. Greats were now very much on my horizon and I was worried that I was spending too much time with Belinda. And so I broke off our liaison. Tears flowed on both sides. I felt like a cad. This break-up was just as bad as the break-up from Jenny. And I fear that it was no better for Belinda, even though soon afterwards she met the man she married.

Ken and I had our tutorials together. With Richard Robinson for philosophy. We handed essays to him in alternate weeks, and read them out in alternate weeks. It was never very clear that he either read them or listened to them. For when a reading was finished he immediately went on to another subject, and he never wrote any remarks on our essays apart from Beta + for Ken and Beta + ? + for me. I was rather tickled by my extra ? +. Peter Brunt for ancient history was totally another matter. He was a small man with a pot belly and delightfully enthusiastic. He listened, was encouraging, and made pertinent and constructive comments. He wrote his own essay on our essays; the only problem was that I could not decipher his handwriting. Perhaps I was too lazy myself. For many years now I have regretted not concentrating on periods of ancient history that I had not studied at school. I was too intent on achieving a First, and not enough on thinking things out for myself – something which I certainly did for Pindar. I had one other tutor just for a term, Willie Abraham, a Ghanaian studying for his PhD in Philosophy at All Souls. I was very impressed and delighted to be a pupil of a native Ghanaian, but I found his enthusiasm for the monads of Leibniz difficult to understand.

21 Vacations

At the start of our second year we were joined by the last of the National Service men. Two became particularly close. Robin Grant had been at Belhaven with me. He was reading history. His father was a Conservative MP in Edinburgh and so we shared many activities in Scotland. We played golf together on the Open Championship course at Muirfield in East Lothian, where he was a member. What I recall particularly were conversations about "the future". Robin had travelled round the USA in a Greyhound bus and learnt a lot. The sight on our way to Muirfield from Inveresk of a dump at Prestonpans covered with clapped-out, rusty cars started an important conversation, a conversation that was probably the conceptual seed for what I am now writing. Robin had been introduced to the books of the American social journalist Vance Packard, *The Hidden Persuaders* and *The Waste Makers*. Packard was deploring the waste-making, money-making, planned obsolescence, and hidden psychological manipulation used to encourage people to buy and replace material goods that they did not actually either need or even want. Through them I began to realise that the wartime and post-war ideal of thriftiness was giving way to a world that depended on the making of goods, whether or not they were needed. Robin was also a keen and good hockey player, as was another Belhavenite, Bruce Patullo, who had come up to Hertford College to study agriculture and who I much enjoyed meeting from time to time. Another new hockey player for Oriel was Adam Raphael, who immediately struck up a friendship with Ken and, by association, with me. He and Ken were Londoners and shared many interests. They were tennis players; I was a cricketer. I think they saw me as an inexperienced young Scot who needed to be brought along. They were both the proud owners of scooters, Ken a Vespa and Adam a Lambretta.

It was in our last summer vac that Adam, Ken, Robin and I decided to go in Robin's car to see the sites of classical Greece. But that expedition did not happen. Robin and I had gone to a dance in a large house beside the golf course at Muirfield, after which we had planned to play golf before sunrise, the Scottish night being very short and not totally dark. But Robin had forgotten to bring his clubs and so drove back to Edinburgh to fetch them. I waited and waited on the first tee. Eventually I gave up. On returning home I heard that he had fallen asleep at the wheel and had suffered a bad accident. (It was indeed very bad and he never quite recovered in the time that I knew him as a young man.) This sad event led to a change of plan. Between the three of us we had no car, only two scooters. Ken decided to stay at home. Adam bravely offered to take me on the back of his Lambretta. I bravely accepted.

The most difficult part of the journey was from London to catch a tiny air transporter at Deal. A southerly gale with driving rain made the Lambretta feel alarmingly unsafe. Between Paris and Rome we cheated by putting the machine, and ourselves, onto a train. And so we arrived in Rome in the middle of the Rome Olympics. My first ever glimpse of Rome was by night as we rode round a floodlit Colosseum and on, up the Appian Way. Dead tired we slept in a field on the Alban Mount. Perhaps the most amazing aspect of our month's adventure was that we had no arguments until our penultimate night in a hostelry near Brussels. We could have had so many. Adam refused to drink retsina despite its known efficacy against too much fat and oil. The result was that at every hairpin bend in the mountains of the Peloponnese, he was forced to stop and disappear into the bushes. I for my part, on one occasion when we stopped to rest in a layby near Megara, forgot, when we started up again, to put my rucksack back on. And so, on discovering the omission, Adam nobly retraced our route for a full half hour – just in case... But we were extremely lucky. A Greek lorry driver had seen us pull away without the pack, but knew, he said, that we would come back to fetch it. As for the whole expedition, we saw what we wanted: Delphi, Athens, Mycenae, Tiryns, Epidaurus, Pylos, Olympia, a night in Munich Station at the start of the October Beer Festival, and early on after Rome the arid hills and hilltop towns of Southern Italy on our way to the ferry at Brindisi.

There had been other less dramatic trips abroad: to the famous towns of Provence and the Basse Alpes with Gordon Dilworth. It was indeed dramatic when a posse of gendarmes rounded us up while we were eating a picnic lunch in a lavender field. We were held in a cell near Digne and interrogated for a couple of hours. We had the impression that they thought we were Algerian terrorists. Another summer I was taken on as a steward in a small Currie Line cargo boat taking china clay from Fowey to Genoa and picking up marble from Carrara to take to London. There was time to wander round Genoa, amazed that the most fashionable shops were in the narrowest of streets with washing hanging out to dry overhead. The gleaming marble mountains above Carrara were memorable. I failed to find where Michelangelo had hacked out slabs for his statues, but was delighted to eat a delicious meal in the old town of Carrara halfway up the mountain. The wine that washed it down was a most unexpected, icy-cold *amabile* from Orvieto. We also put in at Marseilles, Livorno, Naples and Palermo, enabling me to take quick sightseeing trips to Florence and Pompeii. There was not much work to be done on board, and so I was able to get to grips with Aristotle and Plato. This sea voyage came as a wonderful gift from Rowley Scovell, the Chief Executive of the Currie Line whose son, Kerry, I was tutoring in Latin. On several occasions I stayed at their home near Dunbar and came to know Rowley, Stan and Kerry well. I did a number of other tutoring jobs, which helped to pay for items like golf clubs and indeed rounds on golf courses. I was never the proud possessor of a set of clubs. Such that I had were bought singly and never matched.

22 1960 – Next Steps?
(Population = 3 billion; CO2 ppm – 319; Centigrade – + 0.6)

It was after the trip to Greece that at the beginning of our final year at Oxford, Adam introduced me to Felicity Calderari. She was fascinating, this pretty girl: quarter Italian, quarter Burmese, half English and with some Scottish blood infused into the Burmese. Her family had owned a farm and palazzo in Bofalora on the River Ticino between Milan and Turin. But Mussolini had confiscated the house and the farm did not benefit from an absentee landlord. Felicity's father was born in Burma where his Italian father was doing what Italians did in the nineteenth century; he was following the British Empire as a highly skilled engineer. As a result young Carlo was sent to boarding schools in England. He loved it, both his preparatory school in Dover and his time at Marlborough. He was a superb games player, a huge advantage to a schoolboy in those days. By the time he was fifteen he was playing for Marlborough's first elevens, in both cricket and hockey. Then disaster struck. His childless uncles said to his father, "Ignazio, your son is becoming too English. If he is to inherit Bofalora from us, he must come home to Italy." And so he left Marlborough. He was sent to a Swiss school, where his only exercise was walking in crocodile to church.

He never really recovered. He lost his motivation. He fought on the Italian front in World War I, but as soon as he could he married an American heiress (he was very handsome) and they settled in Richmond, Surrey. There he played cricket and hockey to his heart's content. His wife bore him two children, but the elder boy suffered from Down's Syndrome and the younger was killed in the Ardennes in 1944. And the marriage was not a success. Carlo married his boys' governess, Joyce Storey, and they had two girls, Carol and Felicity. To some extent Carlo, now Charles, liked his time in the Second World War where his fluent Italian and French were useful to Monty's intelligence unit. But like all service-aged men at that time he wasn't often at home. Felicity adored him. When I met Felicity, her family had just bought (with what was left of the Bofalora estate) a part of a very pretty villa in Rapallo on the Italian Riviera. The Italian Riviera resonated with me, not just because I was studying Roman literature and history, nor just because of my mother, but because I had an image of all the artists and poets who had congregated there. Felicity's sister, Carol, had also recently married Franco, a Milanese architect, much against her parent's wishes. Though still living a couple of months a year in Italy, Charles and Joyce (especially Charles) did not like the suffocating style of family life there. Felicity meanwhile was working in the John Radcliffe Hospital in Oxford as a trainee cardiac technician, sharing a large shabby flat with friends in North Oxford. Her parents were living near Winchester while Charles had a post in Twyford School teaching languages and sport. Felicity took me to meet them one weekend late in March after my penultimate term at Oxford. I remember vividly a wonderful walk we did together in the fresh spring sunshine over Twyford Down into the Itchen Valley and through the grounds of Winchester College, its great plane trees still bare, finally reaching the Bishop's palace where Felicity's old boss,

Commander Jack Baker, worked as the Bishop's secretary. The Bishop's palace, the seventeenth-century Wolvesey Palace, complements Winchester College's austere late medieval grandeur. It was a very happy weekend.

But with Finals looming close by, I was looking ahead to life after university. I did not really know what path I wanted to take; in those days little advice was given. Shipping? I liked the idea of a career that spanned the world, and I had connections through Rowley Scovell and in the Ben Line where distant cousins were in charge. But British shipping was in crisis because of the increase in air travel, nor had container ships yet been invented. Rowley Scovell was not encouraging. I also toyed with joining a young group helping to house war refugees stuck in middle Europe. This would be a temporary post and my answer to National Service, which had ended the year before. My parents thought that I should just get a proper job.

But then I had an offer out of the blue. I think Peter Brunt was the intermediary. Would I care to go to Massachusetts to Groton School for a year? An English classics teacher, Hugh Sackett, was taking a sabbatical to do archaeological work in Crete. The school was looking for a temporary replacement and since one of its alumni was studying physics at Oriel, the search started there. Though I was not a great admirer of the USA, I jumped at it. I would receive a good salary, board and lodgings, and – after all – I was not unacquainted with boys' boarding schools. Groton was a top American school, counting Franklin D. Roosevelt as one of its alumni, not to mention other Democrat luminaries. This was going to be my equivalent of National Service. I could afford to take the year off, and I would have a change from Great Britain, which I still thought from time to time was a gloomy and parochial place.

But Finals had to be taken, and Felicity and I had to sort things out. We decided that we did want to be married, and the post at Groton would probably provide a good springboard. The parents of neither of us were convinced, but their objections were muted. A final decision would not be taken until I had spent at least one term at Groton and she had got into her final year at the Radcliffe. In the meantime after Finals, together we went to the Magdalen College Commemoration Ball.

I was not very confident about my exam results. I thought that I had written decent papers in ancient history, but not better than that. Philosophy I had always found difficult. I was interested in Plato and Aristotle. I could put them in a context. But racing through the British empiricists, having started with Descartes, and finishing up with A. J. Ayer, Wittgenstein and the Logical Positivists, I lost my way, even to the extent of doubting my own existence! Perhaps it would have helped to have had a tutor who had engaged me more than Richard Robinson. But, as is always said, universities are more important for their paid thinkers than their paying students. In the end I achieved a Second, the equivalent of a 2.1 nowadays. Ken and Adam achieved the same. Robin, not surprisingly, got a Third.

And so to the United States of America.

EARNING A LIVING, 1961–1967

23 Travel

Mum and Dad saw me off on *The American Importer*, which was waiting on the Clyde. She was a small cargo boat with steel decks and small cabins. There were eight passengers bound for Boston, Massachusetts; four ladies, who seemed old to me, and four of us under the age of thirty-five. I did not know what the boat was carrying apart from Scotch whisky. Coming from near Edinburgh I had never known how close Glasgow was to the Scottish Highlands, but as we slipped down the Clyde at a leisurely speed on that overcast September evening, I was fascinated by the lochs opening up to the north and west with high, dark hills on either side of them. But once we passed into the open sea, the movement of the ship changed. We went straight into a storm blowing at a hundred miles an hour, the remains of Hurricane Betsy. I did not quite realise this, until having had breakfast we younger ones went on deck holding onto the rails as the boat went into great frothing waves and bucked and twisted between occasional glimpses of the rocky North Irish coast. The passengers soon took to their cabins and did not appear again for two days. George Gibb and I were exceptions. George had travelled much and was used to rough seas. I had had experience in the Bay of Biscay. But even we succumbed briefly to the sea's force. I remember reading *Death in Venice* and feeling distinctly queasy. The voyage was scheduled to take eight days. In the end it took fourteen since Hurricane Betsy was followed by the remains of Hurricane Louise. American cargo boats are dry but the captain took pity on his passengers and sent down two large bottles of gin, which were gratefully received. Then at last we were sailing in calmer waters, along the gloomy coast of Newfoundland. And a day or two later we put into Boston. I passed through customs and immigration – easily. A day at the American Embassy in London had been well spent and I had been able to swear that I had never been a Communist. Groton had also provided all the necessary documents about my appointment. On this sunny day in Boston they had sent a taxi to meet me, driven by Bucky who, I soon got to know, was an important part of the Groton community.

24 Groton School, Massachusetts

The village of Groton and the boys' school close to it lie west of Concorde and near Massachusetts' border with New Hampshire. It was, and is, a very good-looking school, built of red brick and white clapboard. Only the gothic chapel is constructed of stone. Its magnificent tower furnished with a peal of eight large bells cast in London's Whitechapel foundry make it an unusual feature in the USA. Groton was indeed founded with England in mind by the Rev. Endicott Peabody. It is an Episcopalian school and takes its religion seriously, but not fanatically. Peabody was its first headmaster and reigned for fifty years. Jack Crocker, also a Reverend, succeeded him but after twenty-five years was nearing the end of his time. He was a very impressive man: tall, white-haired, fine-featured, with a deep, modulated voice. His views were liberal and clear, though not ahead of his time. I shall never forget the first faculty meeting that I attended at the end of my first term. This meeting took place at the end of every term after all the boys had departed and lasted a full working day and more. Every one of the 250 pupils was discussed, often at great length. The school was meant to be a family to the extent that each pupil was well known to all the teaching staff. We were discussing a particular boy who I had got to know, a boy who was timid and vulnerable. He was too often open to ridicule, especially from a rather bigger boy in the same year. I was trying to describe the situation (in my very English voice) and said: "The ****** in the woodpile is…" Suddenly the packed room fell totally silent… But Jack Crocker? He gave out a soft boom: "Jock, we don't say that sort of thing round here". And normality was restored. At the end of that session, which was the last of the day, two bachelor teachers, who were as new as me and had become friends, could not, as we went away together, help bursting into fits of giggles at my terrible gaffe in this liberal school. A year or two later Tim Towell had entered the Diplomatic Service, eventually to become an ambassador, and Bill O'Donnell had fallen out with Jack Crocker who suspected him of being gay.

I learnt a lot at Groton. Not so much from the workings of the school, where junior faculty members were rather like prefects at Glenalmond in that they looked after dormitories divided into cubicles. Indeed my bedroom was all but a cubicle and my study was the before-bedtime playroom for twenty thirteen-year-olds. Nor indeed from the daily routines of academic classes and sport. But I did learn to coach the American version of soccer, and play the American hard-ball version of squash, and also to coach baseball. In Latin and Greek I had a breakthrough with literature, largely the result of an American book on Horace's Odes by Brooks Otis who went into fine and interesting detail on poetic wordplay and rhythm and how they deepened meaning, subjects which British schools at that time in their drive to teach ancient languages mostly eschewed. I found the boys at Groton to be quick and intelligent learners; which also taught me a thing or two.

There were many interesting and unusual members of the faculty. One was Ernst Loewenberg, who with his family had escaped the Nazi persecution of the Jews just before the Second World War. They were all so hospitable to this young British immigrant. Also Melvin Mansur and Norris Getty, my fellow classicists, both not far from retirement. Melvin should have included Russian in the subjects he taught. His Russian wife, Lida, had escaped from Stalin and they and their three daughters spoke Russian within the family. Norris was a pure large-boned American, an astute Greek scholar from Iowa. George Zink was a biochemist who took me bird-watching early in the morning to the marshy fields near the Nashua River. He was interested in what I had learnt about the Mind at Oxford and was convinced that the way forward was not by following the paths described by Descartes, Hume, or A. J. Ayer, but by examining the synapses in the brain.

Zen Buddhism was another new subject. I had become friendly with two brothers, Jacques and Nicholas Seronde who on finding out that I liked hill-walking persuaded their dad to take them and me into the Monadnock mountains. The mountains, I thought, were dull. There were no views; there were too many trees, not like my beloved Scottish Highlands. But the conversation was far from dull. Mr.

Seronde was very interested in Zen and how important it was in the rush of modern life. He introduced me to Alan Watts' book *The Way of Zen,* which in turn introduced me to Hinduism and mainstream Buddhism. And that, in turn, connected me to my early years in India.

Days off and holidays were spent in exploration. Bill took me to see the dazzling colours of the fall in New England and cold March days on Cape Cod, so vividly caught by the bleak tangibility of the paintings by Andrew Wyeth. I visited Boston and heard the Boston Symphony Orchestra, famous for the precision of its stringed instruments. And at Christmas time, George Gibb and I went with his friend Beth down to New Orleans. This took place just after Felicity and I had decided to have our engagement announced in *The Times* of December 21. On our way we stopped in Birmingham, Alabama at the house of a medical friend of Beth's. And so we learnt all about "the inevitable woes, still to come", of the NHS in Britain and in the USA "the absolute necessity of racial segregation". George had another friend in New Orleans where we stayed for five nights over Christmas. On the 21st, the day when the *Times* was due to include our announcement, I was delighted to spot that our tram to the centre of Orleans was passing down Felicity Street, a good omen, I thought, for the future. I was fascinated by New Orleans: most obviously the trees covered with Spanish moss lining the avenues, the abundance of magnolias and camellias in the middle of winter, and the quaint Hispano-French houses in the Quarter with iron grills on their balconies – and the jazz.

After our return to the deep snow, bright blue sky, and freezing temperatures of New England, the winter began to thaw slowly at the end of March. And by the start of the summer term at the beginning of April, the spring had arrived. Jack Crocker had been very kind to keep me on for an extra year because the archaeologist, Hugh Sackett, was still excavating in Crete. He allotted Felicity and me a well-constructed, convenient house and added 50 per cent to my salary – and I no longer would have any duties as a dormitory master. Could I be luckier than that?! I must have been so intent on my work and forthcoming return to England to be married, that I cannot remember if I even noticed the news about the fiasco at the Bay of Pigs. More immediately I was amused (I don't think that I should have been) by the boys' reactions to my defence of even the existence of the Labour Party in Britain.

Some of them were appalled that they were being taught by a Communist. But this Communist did deign to visit the Groton Town Meeting. Dealing with all manner of local matters, it was packed and vibrant.

25 Marriage

In the middle of June I flew back to England in a Britannia from Boston airport. Night scarcely fell and I was able to see Greenland and Iceland before we flew into the damp of Shannon Airport. A quick hop across Ireland and the Irish Sea and the plane landed at Heathrow, where not many years earlier archaeologists had found a Roman villa. England felt very small and crowded. Scotland less so. But they were both cold. Dad now gave me for our wedding a small, second-hand, grey Mini, a make of car that had only recently come onto the market. In this I could zip down to Padbury, near Buckingham, where Felicity's parents now lived and zip back north again. It was very different from the large, bulbous, black Ford that Norris Getty had sold me when I first arrived in Groton.

Padbury was a quintessential English village with white, black-beamed, thatched houses. The whole village was owned by All Souls College in Oxford. Preparations for the wedding were well advanced. We were to be married in the village church at Swanbourne where Felicity's godfather, Harold Evans, was the headmaster of the prep school. Charles had once taught French and coached cricket there. This year the Australians were touring and Charles was full of cricket chat about what was happening at Lords, or Trent Bridge, or Old Trafford. He left the women to arrange the wedding details. It was Joyce who was in charge. Felicity first had to take her tests and exams as a cardiac technician. They could scarcely have come at a worse time, and she did not do very well. I in the meantime arranged our wedding night at The Rose Revived with its lawns sweeping down to the gently flowing Thames.

Saturday August 11 dawned very dark. (Bad light prevented play starting in the Fifth Test.) I had been staying the night at The Blackbird in Padbury and drove from there to Swanbourne with David Hart, an usher and a good friend from Glenalmond. We passed a funeral on the way, which I knew would not have pleased my mother. But the service went well. Felicity arrived looking wonderful in the white gown that she herself had made. Photographs showed me looking rather solemn. I made a reasonable speech and mentioned Felicity Street in New Orleans. Then we drove off to The Rose Revived and were relieved that nobody had attached anything strange to the car. But when we arrived at The Rose Revived, there was no room for us. Somehow it had been cancelled. And there was no way to overturn the cancellation. The management instead booked us into a hotel in Witney and paid half the cost. Witney in those days was famous for its blankets, but the hotel was cold and empty.

The next day the sun shone. We flew across the Channel from Deal and made our way to Brittany along small, straight French roads in our grey Mini. We ate and drank well, visited markets and failed to understand much of what the Bretons said to us. At the little Le Touquet airport, waiting for the tiny plane to fly us back over the Channel, we celebrated with two glasses of Dubonnet. Not much later, after a night staying with the Bakers in Winchester, Charles saw us off at Southampton docks. We were sailing in the *Saxonia*, a Cunarder that took us to Montreal, a journey that included a quick visit to Quebec. The voyage this time was uneventful, but our two-berth cabin was pokey. I had to be philosophical about not affording a better one.

We were met in Montreal by Charlie Sheerin, the Groton chaplain who came originally from Charlottesville in Virginia. He was a real romantic southerner who could not restrain his tears when watching Gregory Peck in *To Kill a Mockingbird*. He and his wife, Edith, had a house in Vermont, where they lived throughout the long summer vacation. That was where he took us. Almost as soon as we were on the road Charlie had to pull the car over onto the grass verge because a whole clapboard house was being transported in the opposite direction. Felicity was delighted. Her father, remembering his experiences of the 1930s, had always promised that we were bound to see such a sight in the USA. She also loved the wild animals that lived all around the Sheerin's house. Chipmunks were everywhere, Edith's dog had recently been wounded by a porcupine, and there was a woodchuck burrowing under the house.

The next day we arrived in Groton. Our house, our very first house, was wonderfully neat and tidy and more than sufficiently large, and the next few days were punctuated by faculty wives bringing us small house presents. Sometimes they weren't so small. We acquired an elegant octagonal card table, and not the sort with a baize surface. It did duty as a substantial table for the dining room. It enabled us to entertain. There were a number of new temporary members of the faculty, mostly bachelors. There was David Koth, having a change from his school in Elizabeth, New Jersey; Evaert van Buchem, filling in for Norris Getty. Evaert came from Nijmegen in Holland. Bill O'Donnell was still around, as was Tim Towell. A young American from Ohio was also new, Robert Schneider. He used to flirt with Felicity, which made me uncomfortable. Various families invited us to meals: the Sheerins of course, Jake and Sandy Congleton, and the Rimmers. It was noticeable that the married members of the faculty entertained us as a couple, although they seldom had entertained me on my own. Felicity was a great draw, and on her own initiative she made friends with Lida Mansur and her Russian-speaking daughters.

My teaching was now more relaxed and more focussed. I had taken over Norris Getty's classes and his classroom. It was a big, light-filled room (a change from a smaller dark one) and every time I entered I could smell its pine dados and the polish on the large rectangular table, which I used for small classes and tutorials. I loved teaching these young, intelligent Americans. They devoured the Odes of Horace and *The Histories* of Herodotus. I probably taught better now that my evenings were not continually interrupted by boys in a dormitory.

This was the time when American soldiers were beginning to move into Vietnam. A couple of families had young men being drafted, which they viewed with apprehension. It was in October too that the Cuban Crisis erupted. Again, I can hardly remember noticing it. What were Felicity and I doing!? At about that time we visited Old Sturbridge Village, a working model of a seventeenth-century village with watermills driving lathes for the production of finely made wooden bowls and implements. Soon, after that visit, winter suddenly arrived. A small lake in a sheltered valley near the school froze over so suddenly and completely that its ice was smooth and dark and could withstand any number of tumbles and crashes. Felicity had never skated before, though I had – just a little – in East Lothian.

It was particularly during the holidays that we were able to explore. At Thanksgiving we saw the sights of New York for three days, going round the wonderful art galleries, up the Empire State building, and to the theatre, taken by the Greek mother of a pupil of mine, Peter Goulandris. But we stayed at Groton for a friendly, fairytale white Christmas with the snow lying two feet deep and the sun shining in a bright blue sky. And then when spring came, we went south to Williamsburg, Washington and Charleston.

26 Staying On

We were fascinated by the United States and decided to stay on for an extra year when our time at Groton came to an end. That meant looking for a one-year post. Interviews at St. Paul's School, New Hampshire and St. George's, Rhode Island stopped abruptly when I said that we would stay for only one year. But St. Andrew's, Boca Raton, Florida was different. We went to New York to meet Father Wyatt-Brown, the headmaster and founder of this new school. He was very keen to have us. I think that he took a particular fancy to Felicity. I explained that we would probably stay for only a year, but he was determined that we would so like it and the salary he was offering was so big that we would stay on longer. And so the deal was done.

Now we had a whole three-month summer vacation to fill. We would go on a mammoth tour in our old beat-up Ford accompanied by Evaert van Buchem. Marjory Peabody, the daughter of Endicott, thought that this wasn't good enough. We should take a better car, her own car, a big, dependable Dodge Pioneer. "It needs to go on vacation like you!" she said. "It needs a change from its normal dull life." We were amazed and accepted.

We were away for two months. Many were the sights we saw. Brown bears scavenging uncomfortably near our small tent in the Appalachians. Coal mines and caves in West Virginia. New Orleans again. Greek styled plantation mansions on the Mississippi. Rattle snakes rattling and woodpeckers pecking in the Austin State Park. A dentist in Houston and nodding donkeys nearby. Deserts and mountains, mountains and deserts on our way to the baroque churches of Queretaro and Mexico City. The Toltec temples at Teotihuacan. Deserts and mountains on our way back to the USA and Albuquerque. Desert and petrified forests on the way to the Grand Canyon. Hummingbirds and huge white cliffs in Zion National Park. The desert in Nevada. The lake formed by the Colorado River near the burlesque strippers of Las Vegas. Photosynthetic smog in Los Angeles. Pelicans and a dangerously cold sea on the middle Californian coast. The cool city of San Francisco, up-and-down hills, a Chinatown and the Golden Gate. Falling asleep at the wheel after drinking wine in the warm Napa Valley – saved by Evaert. Redwood Forests and heavy rain. Deer and snowy mountains in the Olympic National Park. Lunch at the top of Seattle's Needle. An English game of bowls in Victoria, Vancouver Island. Goods trains, a hundred trucks long, winding through the Rockies. Moose grazing on the bright green slopes halfway up the Grand Teetons. Geysers, bears, and black squirrels in Yellowstone. Buffalo in South Dakota. Women in grey dresses and men in black stove-pipe hats, Menonites picnicking by a lake in Wisconsin. *The Death of a Salesman* in Minneapolis, and Evaert developing a sore throat from talking Dutch for the first time in a year. Friendly travelling salesmen in Chicago. A production line for Ford cars in Detroit. Natural gas to cook by on the shores of Lake Erie. Floating logs in Ottawa. Speaking French in a cold Quebec. Coffee and biscuits with a Dutch woman on an island in the St. Lawrence River. On the island of North Haven off the coast of Maine staying in the Crockers' sunny holiday home. The Wrights' holiday home by a large lake in New Hampshire. And back to Groton. And that was not quite the end because we had accepted an invitation to stay on Long Island with Corky Nichols at his house by Oyster Bay. There we sailed in Long Island Sound with the thought of Tom and Daisy Buchanan looking out over the water in *The Great Gatsby*. Returning back to Groton for the second time, we became stuck in a traffic jam behind the Labour Day processions in New York.

With considerable sadness we left Groton and its hospitable inhabitants to drive our old Ford and a U-Haul trailer at a steady 40mph south to Florida. We looked in at Savannah and stopped at a motel in North Florida. Its entrance hall was dark and the television was on. I realised it was packed full of people, all of them black, and none of them welcoming. We drove on.

27 St. Andrew's School, Boca Raton, Florida

St. Andrew's was certainly new. Some two miles inland from Boca Raton it was in the middle of flat cactus scrub. An armadillo lumbered across our path as we drove up the road leading to the school. In the school grounds the cactuses gave way to grass, a few pines, and lakes. The white buildings were low, two-storeys high, and attractive. There was a large swimming pool, with tennis courts beside it. The administration building, with its communal, high-ceilinged dining hall, was a focal point. Close by was a simple chapel made out of wood overspread with palm leaves. The weather was very hot and humid, and it had obviously been raining. We were pleased to be shown into our small ground-floor flat in the middle of the long building near the campus entrance. Air conditioning and double-glazed patio doors made the flat deliciously cool. We had been allocated the flat in this building to look after twenty sixteen-year-old boys who lived in small bed-studies along a passage leading away from our flat. There was a similar flat above us and rather larger semi-detached houses at each end of the building. All four living spaces were designed to enable teachers to look after twenty boys. The term was late in starting because not all the building works had been completed. This gave us time to be acquainted with other staff, many of them new like us. We were rather surprised and disturbed to find that Father Hunter Wyatt-Brown was no longer headmaster. He was now concentrating on founding another school further up the coast. He was on a mission to bring education to Florida. The new headmaster was Proc Martin, who for thirty years had been the vice-principal at a school in New York State.

We woke up every morning to a lorry trundling past our bedroom window and settling down to spray clouds of white DDT all over the grounds, the pines, the playing fields and round the buildings. We had just read Rachel Carson's *Silent Spring,* an excoriating account of how this practice was likely to damage not only the mosquitoes and midges, but also birds and even humans. We could, however, see the point of spraying DDT in this part of Florida; otherwise St. Andrew's would have been scarcely habitable. We hoped that Rachel Carson was not right, but we feared that she was. While we walked to the communal breakfast in the heat of the early morning, the DDT still hung in the air. The memory of that has long stayed with me. But at the time reptiles at least were not affected. A huge rattle snake was found very much alive just outside our front door.

Florida has an interesting natural world. There were manatees in the canals not far from the school and alligators lived in the lakes which did duty as hazards for the new golf course down the road. I was warned to be careful when taking a golf ball out of the hole in a putting green; brilliantly coloured, but viciously dangerous, little coral snakes had a habit of curling up in them. In the Christmas holidays we camped in the Everglades and saw all manner of birds from anhingas, pelicans, flamingoes down to tiny warblers. And in the summer we made a trip to Sanibel Island, famous for its shells, on the west coast in the Gulf of Mexico. But it was the East Coast only three miles away that we knew best. There was excellent swimming off bright sandy beaches, with lookouts well placed to watch for sharks and the nasty, purple trails and see-through bulbous tops of Portuguese-men-of-war. A mile or two out it was possible on a calm day to see the Gulf Stream racing north high above the flat sea-surface nearer the land. The golf course at Boca Raton was beside the sea. I played there occasionally, and was much delighted when an old man, watching me practise my swing on the first tee, said, removing from his mouth an old-fashioned metal pipe, "Gee, I haven't seen a swing like that since Tommy Armour!" Tommy Armour was the highly acclaimed professional at Boca Raton and came from St. Andrew's in Fife. I was able to play many rounds of golf because I was put in charge of the golf team; we went to play other schools up and down the coast from Palm Beach to below Miami. The boys were mostly better than me, but they liked my enthusiasm and the fact that I came from Scotland. I was also in charge of debating. This was something I muddled through because it was subject to all sorts of rules and regulations, and I personally was not very good at debating.

What I was good at were the subjects I had to teach. Latin mainly, at a fairly low level. But ancient history too. I enjoyed it and learnt a lot, for we covered Mesopotamia, India, China and Egypt as well as Rome and Greece. I taught one very, very brilliant pupil. Albert Rust. He begged me to teach him Greek in my spare time. In two terms he was able to read Herodotus and Aristophanes fluently; he enjoyed the language and culture so much.

However, the school was not a happy place. The new headmaster was completely lacking in charisma. He dithered over decisions, and often made the wrong ones. Very soon members of the faculty, especially ones in the middle of their career, began to rebel. There were fractious meetings, resignations, and sackings, and finally Proc Martin had to go, with his place being taken by a steady, practical man from Massachusetts. Morale and discipline inevitably suffered. Vulnerable boys were bullied. One boy in my dormitory threatened to commit suicide. I had to see his mother suddenly – after dark (there was no father). She was very anxious, had drunk too much, and kept swearing at her non-existent husband. Finally she grabbed my testicles and tried to kiss me. I beat a rapid retreat as best as I could. But the boy did come through his depression. There were many unsettled people in that part of Florida, which did not help the school in its troubles. Nevertheless, we came to know well a number of fellow teachers and their partners. Joe Gould was a most interesting retired history professor of a small college in Illinois. He specialised in American history and was knowledgeable about modern democratic politics. As I was in his department for teaching ancient history, we had opportunities for long, purposeful conversations.

In the middle of the troubles over the headmaster, on an unusually cloudy November day, news suddenly came through from Dallas that President Kennedy had been assassinated. It was an awful day and did nobody's morale any good. In the end it probably contributed to us keeping to our decision to stay only one year at St. Andrew's despite our earnings now being close to $8,000 per annum, not to mention the free board and lodgings during term time. The reason for this large income was that Father Hunter Wyatt-Brown had taken Felicity on as his personal assistant. He really did try to keep us.

28 Next Steps via Rome

Felicity wanted to stay in the USA. The country had given her an escape from a rather tedious life in England. I preferred to return to Britain; I felt I owed it after my subsidised education, but I also thought that while Florida was out on a limb, New England was not. So, I sent letters of application to Phillip's Academy, Andover, where I knew the Head of Classics and also to St. Andrew's, Delaware, which

Melvin Mansur recommended. Groton itself did not have a vacant post, although I was asked back for a permanent post three years later. I also sent letters to Edinburgh Academy, Radley, and Winchester College. All three seemed to want to hear again from me, as indeed did the school in Delaware. Delaware did not seem to have the attractions of New England, and so with some reluctance on Felicity's part I sent long letters to the British schools saying what an excellent teacher I was. Without an interview I received an offer from all three. Oh, dear! What to do! I chose Winchester, Felicity's least favourite. She had lived in Winchester. She had had a brilliant boyfriend in the school who had been cut down by cancer, and she did not want to go back on her tracks. I, on the other hand, knew Winchester to be an unusual school, not just for its academic excellence, but for producing interesting people. I had liked the Wykehamists I met at Oxford, and I was struck by the diverse views of Wykehamist MPs. It mattered to me that as well as right-wing politicians it was capable of sending into the world Sir Stafford Cripps, Hugh Gaitskell, and Dick Crossman, and I was not too put off by Oswald Mosley. And so we prepared to go back to Winchester.

At the end of July, after our friends had given us a warm farewell on the quayside at Fort Lauderdale, we boarded a New Zealand ship bound for Southampton carrying a cargo of frozen lamb. We sailed across the Bermuda Triangle with flying fish spinning through the air beside us before we anchored near Hamilton, Bermuda's main town. We were able to go ashore for five hours, and so we hired bicycles and rode them round the middle of the island in the hot sunshine avoiding huge squashed toads lying on the tarmac. We were amused by the red British telephone kiosks and the tiny cars, and felt strangely at home with loud cricket commentaries coming out of open windows. Back on the ship, there was a canvas swimming pool and a well-stocked bar, and our few fellow passengers were a jolly bunch. We were passing the Needles before we knew it and felt almost sad that we were coming home. Charles was at the dock gates ready to welcome us and soon we were driving up to Buckinghamshire along very narrow, slow roads crammed with traffic.

We had some weeks to spare before the term started at Winchester College. We spent them seeing my parents and friends in Scotland, collecting our Morris Mini Traveller in Newcastle, and driving south to Padbury. We then drove to Dover. I thought it important to see Rome before teaching at the eminent classical school for which I was bound. And Felicity was only too keen to revisit her second native country. After a night in Dover and awakening to the long, loud cries of the seagulls, we reached a small, simple hostelry at Houecourt in Eastern France. Here the central heating was provided in the old manner: our bedroom was above the byre. The next day we crossed the St. Gotthard pass and dipped down to the southern end of Lake Lugano to stay in a less primitive hotel. Then on to Milan for lunch with Carol. I had heard a lot about her architect husband, Franco Bianchi. He had the reputation of being difficult and fussy. Which clearly he was, but he had charm too, about which I had also heard. The two of them lived in a spacious flat in a palazzo that belonged to Franco's family. Franco was very particular about its décor. Carol's role was in the kitchen and at the dining table. After lunch Franco slipped next door to have a siesta before returning to his office. We drove on to Florence, staying in a small pensione near the Duomo. Thence to Rome along the new Autostrada del Sole, which had a section missing between Citta del Pieve and Orvieto.

Though this stretch of road was crowded and tedious for the driver, the high ridge along which we travelled past small farms, vineyards and orchards was very attractive. In Rome we stayed in the Albergo Liberiano, a gloomy hotel near Santa Maria Maggiore. Felicity had discovered a lot from her Wykehamist boyfriend about mid-twentieth-century Italian architects, like Pier Luigi Nervi, and so we went round E.U.R. and the Termini. I was more interested in the Forum and the Pantheon, but we did not omit St. Peters where only recently an unhappy Hungarian had attacked Jesus' mother at the centre of Michelangelo's *Pieta*. We started for home by the coast road, the Via Aurelia, which skirted the marble mountains of Carrara before going over the Appennines at the Bracco pass. Then we arrived at the Calderaris' beautiful apartment in Villa Cosmea above Rapallo, near the steps leading to the church of San Ambrogio. I was enthralled by Rapallo and the lovely Golfo Tigullio enclosed by Portofino and Santa Margherita. No wonder Ezra Pound loved it. Joyce and Charles clearly loved it too, and as a memento of our visit and Felicity's Italian connection, we put on board our little car a beautiful chest, which had come originally from the family seat at Bofalora, made of orange box wood but decorated in Maggiolini style.

Over the next few years from time to time we visited Villa Cosmea. We also visited the farm, which the Calderaris still owned. Prabanasco it was called, beside the clear, fast-flowing River Ticino, famous for fly-fishing and a battle against Hannibal. The day we went there was sunny and clear, but being in the Po Valley its normal weather was fog, according to the last of a long line of family tenants, Mariella and Ernesto. We spent one Christmas in Rapallo, a magical time of warm dark evenings, lighted candles in the churches, and the local Italians taking advantage of the Christmas season to do their shopping in the narrow, blossom-scented alleys, and to see and be seen in the evening *passegiata*. But that Christmas was also sad because the previous Christmas Charles had suddenly died, and so on this occasion Felicity and I drove Joyce to Rapallo in remembrance of him and at a time when she and Charles had not usually gone to Italy. Three years later the farm at Prabanasco was sold to a family of butchers from Magenta. And so the rich soil was turned into grazing for cattle.

29 Winchester College, Hampshire, Settling in, 1964–1967

But in September 1964, we drove back to England, and finally topping a Hampshire down near Easton and aiming straight for the long, low lion-like cathedral, we arrived in Winchester. We had been allotted a three-storey, narrow old town house beside the twelfth-century Kingsgate. We were told that the house had been the guard-house of the gate and that in 1683 after Monmouth's rebellion, prisoners had been held in its cellar for Judge Jeffrey's Bloody Assizes. There was also a story of an underground tunnel linking it with the cathedral. (Prisoners had indeed been held there, but there was no tunnel.) Above Kingsgate there was a beautiful, simple, medieval chapel dedicated to St. Swithun. Repairs to its roof could be made only by workmen coming through our house, up the narrow staircase and out through one of the windows onto the parapet of the gate.

Arriving from the heat and sunshine of Florida, we were in a different world. Not only were we living in a medieval house, but Britain was exciting for its very modernity. Even in Florida the Beatles were all the rage, not just for their music but their youth and looks. And the way people looked in Britain, particularly in London, was startlingly different. Carnaby Street's new fashions had taken off, and posters of Mary Quant could be seen everywhere. Yes, much of Britain still seemed old-fashioned and cramped. The buses and telephone boxes had not changed over the period of our absence, nor had the architecture. That was still to come. But we felt safer in our own country, and delighted by its variety on a small scale, indeed by the small-scale variety of Europe as a whole.

We soon met my College colleagues who were clearly very clever, but lacked the easy charm of the Americans we had known in Groton and St. Andrew's. With our newly acquired American accents we were something of a curiosity, and quickly taken up by the bachelors who had arrived within the last five years. I was somewhat appalled by my academic load. Apart from teaching the *Electras,* one by Sophocles, one by Euripides and the *Choephori* by Aeschylus, I was the form teacher of twelve fourteen-year-old scholars, which meant teaching English literature, the Old Testament, and mid-seventeenth century British history. One of my classical colleagues, an Old Wykehamist, had chosen books for me on these subjects. Normally a form master would have chosen them for himself, but since I had been en route from the USA I had not had the opportunity. The books were very dull and halfway through the term I changed them. I was a form teacher for the next thirty-three years, giving my pupils one lesson, six days a week. In fact I was not called a form teacher; in a typical Winchester way, such a person had the title of div don, "div" being short for "division" and "don" because teachers at Winchester were assumed to be as learned as university dons! In time it was a delightful position; I learnt a lot about literature, world history, world religions, philosophy, art history, and the history of science.

Whether my pupils learnt anything is another matter. The summer holidays were a vital time for preparing courses for these lessons. I did a prodigious amount of reading, much of which was not used in the end but served as a context to what I taught in the classroom. When, after a couple of years, we bought a bolt-hole to use in the summer, a special place in the car had to be found for books.

If my colleagues were somewhat restrained, as indeed I was, my sixth-form pupils, nearly all of them scholars dressed in black gowns, were almost totally silent. Years later two of them confessed. The trouble had been that in studying Greek and Latin literature they were accustomed only to mastering the obscure syntax of different authors. I, on the other hand, influenced by Brooks Otis and others, concentrated on the literary and historical meaning of these ancient works. In time that new method became more usual but it was very strange in 1964. As I had never been interviewed for my position, I was only too conscious that I might not fit the bill. Most of my colleagues had achieved Firsts in their Finals, whereas my lot was a Second. And it was not at all clear that my sixth-form pupils derived any enjoyment from my lessons. One colleague, however, was very helpful. He knew Charles, my father-in-law. They were both Marlburians, and Charles had, I think, asked Richard Bass to look out for me. Which he certainly did. Richard, in turn, also asked me to "look out for" one of my pupils, Tim Wilson, who was in his second year and had very recently lost his father. Tim was a delightful, slightly awkward, clever boy; we got on very well, a friendship that lasted far into Tim's adult years. Richard was his housemaster. He also happened to be in charge of the house where Felicity's previous boyfriend had been, under a different housemaster. So that was a link. Richard was keen that I should not be totally swallowed up by a school that was so demanding. Consequently, I became a visitor at Winchester Prison, a fascinating, but time-consuming, occupation which I carried out on Sunday afternoons. The prisoners who I visited almost to a man came from very poor backgrounds, or, having been in the army, found it difficult adjusting as adults to civilian life. I also became involved, but not very closely, again at Richard's suggestion, with the local Chamber of Commerce. The bank manager of the Winchester branch of Barclays was a leading light in this. It was all very interesting, but on reflection may have been too demanding of my time. During the week I had to prepare my next day's lessons, extra carefully, sitting in my little garret study at the top of the house listening to the mournful tolling of the cathedral bells on Wednesday evenings. Felicity meanwhile was reading or cooking in the small dark kitchen on the ground floor, or visiting friends. Our time together at weekends was limited.

When I wrote to Sir Desmond Lee from Florida I had mentioned that I had played cricket to a reasonable standard, both at school and at Oxford. And so I found myself in the cricket empire of Hubert Doggart, who I remembered had played in 1950 for England against the West Indies. At the same time Charles offered to put my name forward to be a member of the MCC. Charles would have liked nothing more than accompanying his son-in-law to Lords. But somehow I did not fancy it. Felicity's least favourite occupation was anything to do with cricket. I felt rather guilty in declining his offer. But I did try my hand at racquets, a game not unlike squash, but requiring very quick footwork and an even quicker eye. Here I played with the Junior Colts who soon became far better than me. Both cricket and racquets took me to other schools accompanying teams and umpiring their games.

Harry Shaw was one of my pupils in the sixth form, an American boy on a one-year English Speaking Union scholarship. In the early days he was not as silent as his English peers, but he too soon fell silent. When, though, I took him for tutorials (something the school thought important), he was delightfully articulate. Since he was almost of university age, Felicity and I asked him if he would like to accompany us on an expedition round classical Greece in the summer holidays before he returned to the USA. He jumped at the chance, and so, soon after the end of the term, we set off in our Morris Mini Traveller. Felicity had never seen the sites that Adam Raphael and I had visited, but this time we also went to Cnossos and Phaistos, the Minoan cities in Crete. Adam and I had taken the train from Athens to Munich, but this time we motored through Yugoslavia. We particularly admired Lubljana in modern Slovenia. On a very wet night we camped in a pavilion beside a clear-running river full of large, dark trout. Harry left us when we arrived in Venice. We carried on through Northern Italy, camping near the site of Bobbio, a monastery that had been famous for its preservation of medieval and classical manuscripts. We had a strong impression of a far more direct link in Italy with its past history than we had found in Greece. This impression was reinforced in a spring trip the next year accompanied by Joyce, immediately after Charles' death. We stayed in Florence and Certaldo, the birthplace of Boccaccio, and visited the Etruscan town of Volterra. On this occasion it was also obvious that the Italian peasantry were leaving their handsome but primitive houses in the countryside to find work in the cities. The thought then occurred to us – why not try to buy one? As a teacher I enjoyed long summer holidays and it would be good to follow the American practice of owning a summer home. It so happened that in the following term we met Alex Sollohub, the brother of Nick Sollohub, both of whom had fled from Russia with their mother at the time of the Russian Revolution. Nick had come to Winchester to teach Russian after a distinguished time at Dartmouth Naval College; Alex had then started to farm near Spoleto in Umbria before working for the Food and Agricultural Organisation in Rome. He encouraged us and promised to help if we ever put our idea into practice.

The idea took more shape in Scotland. We went to stay with my colleague, Mark Stephenson, who rented for £5 per year a house in the Rough Bounds on the south shore of Loch Hourn. Having picked up Mark in Stirling we arrived at the head of the loch one filthily wet night, and then trudged four miles in the dark along the roughest and wettest of paths slipping and sliding over numerous deep burns, all brown and swirling in spate. Mark lived simply. The toilet was a Racasan in his woodshed. He took water from a burn outside his house, and his rooms were lit by paraffin lamps. It was there that he read many of the books that informed his teaching of history, just enjoying life by the sea and in the hills, catching mackerel in the loch and collecting mussels from the rocks. Thus did he experience a complete change from the close-knit civilisation of Winchester and Winchester College. And so we decided to put our idea into practice, if we could, of owning a simple house in Italy. It would not be easy because sterling was in crisis and we were not allowed to take more than fifty pounds out of the country.

In the meantime I was about to be distracted by a project. The centre of Winchester was full of archaeologists, many of them from the USA. They were uncovering the foundations of the Anglo-Saxon Minsters just north of the cathedral. There were also digs elsewhere in the centre revealing medieval houses and a small Romano-Celtic temple. In the summer of 1966 I went to do some digging and found a number of young Wykehamists doing the same. A few of them came from Richard Bass's boarding house and one evening Richard asked me if I would be interested in conducting a school dig in the grounds of Lankhills Special School, where he was Chairman of the Governors, and where what seemed to be a Roman cemetery had been found. I said I was interested but not very experienced. "No matter," he said. "Some of the boys are acquiring expertise quite rapidly. But there needs to be an adult on the spot." And so it was decided that we would start in the summer term of 1967. I knew that archaeology was one of the pursuits for which Winchester was famous, knowledge that had had some influence on my choice of British school. Names like Noel Myres, Christopher Hawkes, John Pendlebury, Charles Thomas, and more recently Nicholas Postgate were all well known. The first two had actually started their careers while they were still in the school, carrying out an excavation on top of St. Catherine's Hill, a local landmark immediately opposite the city and above the Itchen Valley.

LIVING IN ITALY and ARCHAEOLOGY IN WINCHESTER, 1967–1979

30 Finding Macina, 1967

In April 1967 we put our search for houses in Italy into operation. Felicity and I were joined by Roger Montgomery, a colleague and brilliant mathematician who had become fascinated by Italian art and architecture. To save money I went out on my own. We had agreed that we wanted a house about a mile outside a village on a hillside with a view. Alex Sollohub had agreed to help. So had Di Dowdeswell, the lively daughter of Bunny Dowdeswell, the biologist who was Head of Science. She worked in Strasburg and had agreed to provide us, illegally, with Italian lire, illegally because British people were still not allowed to take more than £50 out of the country.

I reached Paris by train early one morning, took the first train I could to Strasburg and met Di at Strasburg railway station. We drank a coffee together and she handed over the bank notes wrapped up in a brown paper bag. It all felt deliciously covert. I then caught a train to Rome. As soon as I arrived, once again at the Albergo Liberiano, I arranged with Alex to go out to Spoleto. This we did. We visited two house agents, each of whom had a possible house for sale. The first was a wing of an attractive small hill farm complex;

the second was down a very rough track, through a wood, onto a bluff overlooking the Umbrian plain. The house was derelict, and expensive. They were both expensive. It was only later that I realised Americans had moved into the area, because American money was helping to finance the annual festival of *I Due Mondi* in Spoleto.

Alex now had no more time to escort me. He did, however, tell me that he had heard of a house for sale at our sort of price in Civitella d'Agliano, "a most attractive village" in the Tiber Valley not far from Orvieto. And so, after giving myself a crash course in Italian, and learning and practising all the Italian terms that I could find for the business of buying houses, I set off from the hotel on a very wet morning to a little station near the Piazza del Popolo, to board a narrow-gauge train bound for Viterbo. The train rattled round and past the volcanic Cimini mountains. At Viterbo I caught an empty bus to Civitella. The flat countryside of the high Etruscan plain looked unpromising, but the day was brightening up. After half an hour the bus began to descend into the Tiber valley, and here the east-facing slopes looked much more interesting. Alighting from the bus at Civitella, I walked down to the central square of the town which was perched on a steep promontory. The square was surrounded by tall, gaunt, grey habitations. It was not inviting. But that is where I had an address. I knocked. An old man took me to an upstairs flat. We entered a dark bedroom, then passed into a kitchen with rooms off it.

"Here's the apartment," the old man said.

"And the bedroom?" I asked.

"No, that is where we live."

"Oh!" I tried to cover my confusion, and for politeness' sake looked at the other rooms: two bedrooms and a small washroom, without shower or bath. "It's a nice flat. I'll think about it." On leaving the building I asked a woman standing outside a door where I might be able to eat a late lunch. "Here, of course" she said. "I give everyone lunch!" It was a delicious meal: zucchini flowers stuffed with ricotta and anchovies, followed by a large, tasty pork chop and half a litre of a sweetish white wine. I now felt much more cheerful and decided to hitch-hike back to Rome. The sun was shining and the countryside looked sharp and beautiful.

I had walked half a mile up the road when a car stopped. The driver was very friendly. He was the local postman. His name was Umberto. Forgetting completely that I was hitch-hiking to Rome, I asked him if he knew of any houses for sale. "I'm stopping at San Michele, the next village. We'll ask there." The village was smaller than Civitella, and less intimidating. Its square was a wide hairpin bend in the road, with a trough-like fountain against a sunny wall. Apart from two men sitting beside the fountain, the steep sunny street with its small houses was deserted; everybody was having a siesta. But the local policeman, La Guardia, appeared. He had one eye and was easy and informal. Umberto asked if he knew of a house for sale. "I think that Tito, over there by the fountain, may have a house."

Tito was called, and wandered over. "Si, certo! I do have a house. Outside the village. I'll take you there in my car." I thanked Umberto and La Guardia and said goodbye. Tito drove up the steep main street, round two bends and then down where the road, lined by acacia trees, went across a saddle between two hills. We stopped by a tidy grey-washed house in a dusty yard. We walked up a leafy track, which then doubled back. There was the house. It was built of red sandstone and stood square on the side of the hill. It was in shadow, but the afternoon view was beautiful. The Tiber Valley gleamed in the sun and the bluish Umbrian mountains rose gentle but high above it. Straight in front of us was a hillside of olive trees topped by a castle with a single tower. To the right lay a deep valley with a stream and wooded cliffs on the far side. The house had five rooms on two storeys and was surrounded by a level, overgrown space cut into the hillside. There was a storage cave at the back. Birds were singing everywhere.

This was it! "How much?" I asked.

"A million lire."

Six hundred pounds, I calculated. "Done!" I exclaimed, rashly (though I had calculated that we could afford it).

"Done!" said Tito. "Come and drink a drop of wine."

"Yes, please!" We strolled together down the hill and stopped beside another cave behind the lower house. Tito opened the bolted doors and we entered the cool darkness. The cave was full of a wonderful aroma. Tito drew wine from a large barrel into two small tumblers. It was slightly "frizzante", very refreshing, and delicious. And Tito and I arranged to meet the following Sunday to draw up a preliminary agreement on a piece of officially stamped paper. The day had turned out extremely well.

Tito drove me back to the village where he summoned his brother-in-law to take me in his taxi down to the mainline station at the bottom of the valley. There I caught a fast train back to Rome. I remember chatting, fluently I thought, to the people in the carriage. They were amazed that a Scotsman wanted to buy a house in the Tiber Valley.

I had a few days in Rome before meeting Tito again. I went exploring, walking everywhere. I visited small, brilliant baroque churches designed by Bernini, Borromini and Berrettini. The three Bs, I liked to call them. There were also cafés to sit outside and simple meals to eat. I enjoyed myself. I tried to improve my Italian even further.

The following Sunday Alex took me and a middle-aged Russian couple to San Michele in his car. The house was inspected and the large Russian lady said she would not even think of buying the house because the steep drop to the house below would be dangerous for children. When Alex and I did finally meet Tito for the signing of the document, Alex told me to pay no attention to his friend. "She is always forward with her views and it is believed that she beats her husband." The *Carta Bollata*, the stamped document, was duly signed, the money Di Dowdeswell had passed on to me was handed over as a deposit, and we returned to Rome.

31 Romano-British Burials, 1967–1979

Back in Winchester the term started and the archaeology began. With my duties as a cricket coach and responsibilities in the prison, it was difficult fitting in the archaeology. But the archaeology soon became very interesting. The potential of the site had been noticed when a new dormitory for girls was being built. Three graves had been discovered and one of them contained a beautifully fashioned bronze spoon. David Teale, the head of the special school, was most enthusiastic and the arrangement was that some of his more able pupils could take part. Of the Wykehamists, Giles Clarke was in charge, ably assisted by Bryan Ward-Perkins, John Thompson, Simon Esmonde-Cleary and others. The local authorities, Hampshire County Council (who owned the land) and Winchester City Council were most helpful. Tools were provided by the latter and measuring tapes, grids, and other paraphernalia were borrowed from the Winchester Research Unit, headed by Martin Biddle who was conducting his innovative excavations in Winchester itself. From Winchester College, Warden Tuke, the chairman of the Governing Body, and Sir Desmond Lee came to visit. And Richard Bass was always on hand when needed.

That first summer we stripped the topsoil off a small area with our spades in order to find out what lay beneath. Luckily the topsoil was thin at this point and soon we saw the shadows of graves, showing up against the gleaming white chalk, refilled as they had been with brown earth. Quickly it became apparent that the graves did not contain just the people who had been buried in them but also in some cases pottery bowls, coins and even one crossbow brooch. The date on the coins confirmed that it was a fourth century cemetery. And so it was decided that the excavation should be extended both in place and time. The topsoil, which was becoming deeper, was taken away by a mechanical digger in two shifts, after the first year and then before the fourth year, leaving the chalk to be meticulously cleaned with building trowels, brushes and pans. There was also an expansion of those who took part. The two grammar schools (Peter Symonds and the County High), the two Secondary Moderns (Danemark and Montgomery) and the girls' private school, St. Swithun's, all sent interested pupils and occasional teachers. It was usually the case that at the beginning of each summer term there were many teenagers beavering away, making sure that the site was spotlessly scraped and cleaned. By the end of the summer term only the girls and boys who had become particularly enthusiastic were left. It was not until the end of the sixth summer term, in 1972, that the site was finally and fully excavated.

It was in many ways an extraordinary and exciting dig. At the beginning of the final year there were as many as seventy teenagers on the site (although at the end there were scarcely a dozen). Many of them were girls from the three girls' schools who took part: Jane Wadham, Hilary Walker, Suzanne Hughes, and Ros Bignell to name but four who stayed to the end. All over the site there were holes in the chalk with people in them, either scraping away and sifting the soil, or measuring the position of the bones with plumb bob and grid and drawing the skeletons on graph paper for eventual publication. I was the photographer on the site, called on particularly when there were unusual finds, like a gaming set with draft-like pieces, or intertwined bracelets and necklaces, or knives, or belts with dolphin buckles, and crossbow brooches. There were many pots and coins that dated the site and the objects that it contained. There were also seven severed heads. Almost the most extraordinary thing was the energy of the diggers toiling away and pushing wheelbarrows filled with chalk up wooden planks to the top of the tall spoil heaps. And the site was often gleaming hot in the summer sun. If it rained there was shelter under the tall beech trees that flanked one side of the area, or, for a chosen few experts, in the site hut where the records were stored and also the finds before they were taken to a safer home.

By the end of the summer term of 1972 and into the summer holidays, I found myself excavating a particularly large grave that along with other graves lay outside a ditch that seemed to mark a boundary to the cemetery, a boundary that was eventually overrun. These graves on the outside were usually more scruffy and shallow than those inside the boundary. Coins dated them to the early fifth century – at the earliest. The grave that I was excavating was big enough for two of us to scrape away. It was indeed interesting. It was surrounded by a ditch that may have contained a hedge with an entrance at the east end. First we found a skeleton whose head had been decapitated and placed beside his knees. This dead man had been put into the large grave after a period of time, certainly on purpose. Then came the backbone of a dog twisted together to form a sort of crown. Near it was the dislocated leg of a dog. Next, there was a noticeable layer of turf. The grave became deeper. Another dog. This time large and whole with its paws seemingly up in the air. Again deeper. At last, coffin nails. Martin Biddle happened to be on the site at the time and whispered in my ear "Sutton Hoo!" What would be in the coffin? We scraped further. The grave was at least 1.80 metres deep. Then, white virgin chalk. There was nothing at all in the coffin! Apart from five small bronze coins placed where the right hand would have been which dated the grave to some time after AD 400. It was a cenotaph. I have argued elsewhere that it (and six other graves that bore some similarity to it without being cenotaphs) was a ritual burial designed to allow the missing person to cross over into the Other World. The severed head was particularly important in this respect, but the ritual in this cemetery might not have been carried out elsewhere. Indeed the cemetery is unique amongst late Romano-British cemeteries. There were many finds, there were many coins that dated the finds, and there were signs that it contained people that were linked with provinces outside Britain. Giles Clarke wrote up the results of the excavation and completed the work by 1979. His book was hailed as a classic both for its content and for its methodology.

As for the empty grave? It seemed to have a poetic significance. The Roman Empire in the West was coming to an end. The legions and cohorts and foreign mercenaries were leaving Britain. Winchester had been converted, it seems, from an important town into a safe haven and military base camp to protect the south coast from Saxon marauders and would-be settlers. Like the coffin in the grave, the empire in the West had become an empty shell. And the would-be body for the grave may have been killed in warfare.

Some scholars have recently tried to be positive, stressing that out of this chaos came Christianity, or (to support the claims of Germany's centrality to the European Union) that the incomers from beyond the Elbe were the forerunners of a new and vital civilisation. But in fact a civilisation had died. There were no more coins, no more stone houses, no more half-decent pottery, no more clay-tiled roofs. For more than 200 years in Western Europe, human life was short and brutish and even after that it rose only slowly. Bryan Ward-Perkins, who became a don in history and archaeology at Oxford, specialising in this changeover period, made a conclusive demonstration of all that in his masterly short book, *The Fall of Rome and the End of Civilisation*.

32 Macina, 1967–1989

I was hard pressed for time in those early summer terms, with weekends and half holidays spent at Lankhills. Later I gave up coaching cricket, much to the disgust of the permanent cricket coaches. But it was clear after a couple of years that our dig was uncovering something of much greater interest in the long run, and academic interest at that – for an academic school.

That summer term in 1967 was certainly busy – but uneventful, except towards the end. We were planning our journey to our little house outside San Michele in Teverina, known only to me and not yet to Felicity or Roger. My Aunt Eleanor died right at the end of the term. I took the train up to Dunbar and attended her funeral in a wild cemetery outside the town, where the wind blew cold off a choppy sea. Then I went to Oxford for a classical symposium. It was there that Felicity phoned me to say that she was expecting a baby, but she would still come to Italy. I was delighted on both counts.

And so we set off again to cross the channel in our Mini Traveller, having dispatched the money to complete the deal to the Banca di Roma in Orvieto. That included an expensive dollar exchange premium to help us get permission from the Bank of England. The final deed was done in a *notaio's* dingy office in Bagnoregio.

Tito was obviously very pleased with the arrangement. But we were rather annoyed that he had taken away the small lean-to shed behind the house; he had, he said, a use for the stone, tiles, and timbers. We thought that he was something of a wide boy. He had fought in Russia during the war and had escaped from his Italian unit fighting beside the German army. In fact he was usually very helpful, taking us in his car to second-hand stores to buy bedsteads, introducing us to his sister-in-law, Ginevra, who ran the village shop, and being our contact in the village. He was a man to know, a member of the Comune that ran both Civitella and San Michele. He and his wife gave us an excellent Sunday lunch just before we went back to Winchester for the autumn term. The chicken they served us cooked in wild fennel flowers was memorably delicious.

That summer right to the end of our stay was extremely hot and dry. It had not rained for a hundred days. But the water, which came straight out of the hillside into a huge stone laundry trough below the two houses, never failed. We washed our clothes in it, fetched drinking water from it, and even plunged into it. It was icy cold. Every so often water was pumped up from the trough to fill a cistern on one side of our house. From there it flowed down a pipe to the house below. That water was much needed for cleaning the house and whitewashing the interior – and for washing ourselves after a very hard day's work. We just stood under a tap outside the cistern and let the icy water wash the dust off our naked bodies. The building had been inhabited by hens. Time and again we scrubbed, washed, and washed down the grey brick floors to rid them of hen shit. And for years afterwards when we opened the front door to begin our summer stay we could smell a slight but familiar odour. The worst place was "the pong hole" beneath the stairs off the kitchen, closely followed by the domed oven behind the huge, impressive fireplace. The floors upstairs did not help; they bounced as one walked through the two interconnecting bedrooms before arriving at a rather charming tiny room above the oven and cistern. As a rule we worked hard for two days and then spent the third day exploring: Assisi, Todi, Perugia, Spoleto – beautiful Umbrian towns; Rome and Florence, even, and Siena. And all those outstanding Mannerist gardens: Villa Lante, Villa d'Este, Caprarola and the sixteenth-century Monster Park at Bomarzo. I don't know how Felicity survived; she was pregnant with Carlina, something with which she was not entirely happy. A great source of comfort was the proximity of Lake Bolsena, the largest volcanic lake in Europe. It had not been discovered by tourists and its water was crystal clear. Since Roman times it was famous for its eels and *coregoni*, a small fish that resembles a perch. It was also famous for the boat race round its two volcanic islands arranged by the Renaissance Pope, Pius II, in 1448. He was imitating the boat race in the Fifth Book of Virgil's *Aeneid*. What that Pope never mentioned in his diaries, and may not even have known about, was the "monster" in the lake. Every now and again a boat sailing across the lake would disappear. This happened to a friend of a friend who was never seen again, neither he nor his boat. What seems to be the case is that the lake rises and falls about four feet for no obvious reason. But it is a volcanic lake. The volcano is still classed as "active". The best explanation is that vents in its very deep bottom open up and swallow water, and perhaps at the same time a boat. The locals don't like talking about it, but on one occasion we were reading books in a rubber dinghy tied to a fisherman's buoy on a lake that did not display even one ripple on it. But, at a certain moment, I looked up from my book to see a wall of water some two feet high advancing towards us. The rubber dinghy did not capsize but it was a strange occurrence. After a short time the surface of the lake resumed its state of dead calm. All this has made me wonder about the two Scottish lochs, Loch Morar and, more famously, Loch Ness, both of them at least as deep as Lake Bolsena and known for their "monsters". Their depth is the result of geological faults, which could, I suppose, shift from time to time and cause disturbance on their surface.

We learnt a lot that first summer. And it was not just about art, architecture, history and volcanoes. We experienced the last days of a form of agriculture that stretched back to the Ancient World. Every morning we heard a creaking sound approach us. And there came Gianni Teodori in his wooden cart, drawn by two huge, low-geared, and dazzlingly white oxen. Once there was a great shuffling noise right outside our house and a team of six white oxen passed us, pulling a sledge loaded with tree trunks from the forest far below us on the left. Gianni worked for Tito. I think that between them they used the ancient *mezzadria* system, whereby a tenant would give half the produce from his plot to the landowner and keep the other half for himself and his family. Gianni's wife, Maria, was constantly lamenting her poverty, though her five handsome children brought up mainly on a vegetarian diet were healthy and strong. But these children, like so many other rural Italians, did not remain in the village; instead they went to find work in Milan 300 miles away.

Macina faced south-east, so that its front wall was scaldingly hot in the morning. It was best to keep inside. The sun went off the wall at precisely two-twenty every day. It was cool in the lower rooms as the walls were over one metre thick, but the three interlinking bedrooms were hot at night. Once the house was tolerably cleaned and whitewashed inside, Felicity used those mornings during which she had to stay inside to paint a beautiful Madonna and Child after Cimabue at the top of the staircase that went up along the inside of the front wall of the house.

The house complete with that painting was sold exactly fifty years after we bought it. Felicity took it over as the sole owner when she and I separated in 1989, though she still allowed me to use it from time to time. But until 1998 Roger lived there like a hermit during the winter from September till June, vacating it only to give us two months of enjoyment. There were some benefits from this odd arrangement. He built up the vegetable garden with topsoil that had dropped over the cliff from the hill behind the house. It was very fertile and he was able to live mainly on its produce, leaving some for us to glean when we came in July. His little tomatoes were deliciously sweet, as were the carrots. He made an asparagus bed and a potato patch; zucchini and melanzane grew in great profusion; there were even strawberries. The hillside had a reputation for fine fruit even before we came, and so there were trees with cherries, pears, and figs all around.

Roger did not bother about the fabric of the house. That was left to me. He was able to survive on an expenditure of less than £1,000 a year. But he so depended on his vegetables that when a radioactive cloud spawned by Chernobyl stopped overhead, he disregarded the local advice not to eat produce from the ground. As a result, maybe, he contracted the bowel cancer that eventually killed him.

The children, particularly Alessia, who was five years younger than Carlina, loved their Italian house. There was always great excitement when, after a three-day journey from Winchester, we first saw it as we started descending the road that wound past the castle. But our first task, one that Carlina and Alessia did not like, was to clean the house and make up the beds. Then, filthy with dust, off we would go, to the lake to soap ourselves down before having a special supper at the very highest point of Montefiascone, on – as it were – the rim of the volcano's crater. From here we could watch the sun set over the western rim. The summer heat meant that we always had a siesta after lunch. But when the heat began to dissolve in the late afternoon, to cries of "Can't we go now, Dad?" the lake beckoned again: to swim, to play pig-in-the-middle in the water, and to read. Then there were ice creams, delicious locally made ice creams in a special café. Sometimes we used to go to Rome for the day, or Assisi, often taking friends who did not know that part of Italy. Then when the sun still shone on the Umbrian hills beyond the Tiber we would sit on the uneven basalt steps outside the front door watching the shadows slowly grow up the slopes or the swallows gathering on the telephone wires for their autumn departure. Once we saw a flight of swallows circling a large olive tree on the hillside opposite. With them was a white bird that we could not identify. Round and round they went until with the sun almost setting behind us they dispersed. Finally we knew what the white bird was. It came steadily towards us. Twice it wheeled gracefully over the house as if to salute us. It was a white swallow.

Other memories: bats coming out of a hole beneath the smallest bedroom. One bat, two bats, three bats – the children started to count them, and so did I; ten bats, twenty bats, forty bats, eighty bats, and finally one hundred and twelve bats. All from under the floor of the smallest bedroom. Snakes too lived round us. Big green or black grass snakes. One or two small vipers, enough for us always to stamp hard on the ground when going into the garden. One morning when I arrived back from Fiumicino Airport at sunrise, after friends had failed to turn up on a late plane, and I was walking up the path, a distance of a hundred yards, I was astonished to find that, at almost every footstep, out shot snakes – big snakes, small snakes, medium-sized snakes. Arriving at the house somewhat shaken, I lay down on my bed and went to sleep only to be woken up by Carlina bumping my bed. No, it wasn't Carlina. It was an earthquake.

The wild life on that hillside was abundant: hoopoes calling "u-poop, u-poop", golden orioles, their cries and the females' plumage scarcely distinguishable from the green woodpecker's, owls echoing at night in the valleys, red kites, black kites, booted eagles, buzzards mobbed by hooded crows, red and grey shrikes, and in the undergrowth all manner of warblers, robins, hedge sparrows and nightingales who were only to be heard in springtime. Latterly, there were new summer migrants coming up from the south, chief of which were the bee-eaters, long-billed and gloriously coloured, who our local Italians called "*rondini di mare*", sea swallows, because of their soft, mellifluous cries. There were animals too. We kept on finding desiccated hen feathers until we realised they belonged to porcupines. During our time wild boar became increasingly common, and once, when I was sitting by myself on the house steps, a dog fox came up under the fig tree, and, standing on its hind legs, nipped off a fig, just to show that the ancient Greek and Roman artists really did have an accurate eye for the elegancies of nature. Another time, sitting in the same place, I heard a tremendous rattling coming down the path in front of the house. There, just below me, hurtled, extremely fast, one of those big, brilliantly green rural lizards; and following it, at a much more leisurely pace, but somehow catching up, was an enormous grass snake. To my delight the lizard made its escape.

But the countryside was not entirely idyllic. The migration of rural people to the big cities left many little fields and plots abandoned. The vines straggled on their small, supporting trees, the weeds and grass grew lank and dry, forests burnt, and rich townies moved in to build villas that were usually tastelessly ostentatious. We were also afraid that in an effort to halt the trend the Italian government would drive a large road past us linking the port of Civitavecchia to the main Florence to Rome motorway. Eventually a road was built but further south, past Viterbo.

Twenty years went by before the exodus began to be reversed. New vines were planted for "Orvieto wine", vines that were now trained on modern wires supported by clean-shaven posts, no longer in the old Roman way on little trees, but better than desert scrub. Europe may have been suffering from a "wine lake", and no doubt European money supported these new vineyards, but they had the great advantage of holding the land together. Even slopes that resembled the Badlands of South Dakota were planted with vines and became brilliantly green instead of a dirty white.

But before all this happened, Tito wanted to get much more money from his land. His first venture was to rent it off to a family of Sardinian shepherds. There were three of them: a man and his wife, and a sister who was a nun, robed in black. The sheep bells were a joy to hear and the flock as it roamed around caught the eye. But my main memory was of one hot afternoon, when the pregnant wife seemed to be on her own, and we heard dreadful, agonising cries coming from the house below. I went down the path to find out the cause. I saw the woman standing motionless, holding her belly, beside a small improvised hen house. When she saw me, all she could do was to point and wail. I looked at the direction she was pointing, and there, in a rough hen's nest was a very large toad squatting beside an egg. No doubt the poor woman took this as an ill omen for her unborn child. I fetched a stick, prodded the toad out from its comfortable position, and then bowled it down the slope with my makeshift hockey stick. Down it rolled like a semi-deflated football.

33 An Uncomfortable Neighbour

Finally, Tito sold the house below and all the land we could see in front of us to a Neapolitan engineer named Giuseppe de Filippis, and that was the beginning of a six-year saga. In the spring of 1971 Roger wrote us a typically ironic letter: this intruder had stripped the slope between the two houses of all vegetation, and had filled it with clucking hens, squawking guinea fowl, and the piercing cries of a forlorn and bedraggled peacock. The slope was now an arid, dusty desert surrounded by lopsided chicken wire. De Filippis had also decided that his straightforward farmhouse and its accompanying pigsty should be turned into a large, white Spanish hacienda. To make quite sure that everyone knew that he had arrived, he had erected a monumental gate beside the road at the end of his short drive. Roger was writing a novel, and he did not like his concentration being disturbed by squawks and piercing cries, nor his idyllic view being interrupted by a dustbowl and a huge barren red roofscape.

We arrived for our summer break. It was as he described, and it soon became clear that de Filippis wanted us OUT. He offered to pay us a small price for the house to help us buy another one. In order not to snub him totally, we did go through the motions of trying to find another. But prices had gone up and we could honestly say that he had to double his offer. He was not prepared to do so; instead he started to cut off our road with a hired bulldozer. We remonstrated with him. We contacted Tito. Tito brought the matter to the attention of the Comune. And the Comune said that de Filippis had to make us another road. This he did, reluctantly. So instead of going past the lower house as we had done ever since our purchase, we now had our own track leading straight up the gradual slope of the hill from the public road. The outcome was good. But de Filippis had not finished. He now tried to drown us. He started pumping so much water into the cistern inside the house that it overflowed and soaked the walls. What was almost worse, he destroyed the big cistern at the bottom of the hill with its laundry slabs and icy water three metres deep. No longer could we use it even to draw drinking water. Perhaps in this instance he had some justification. Felicity, as was her custom, had taken the household washing down the hill to the cistern. She had completed her task, but within the hour the *ingegnere*'s fine ornamental mare had drunk the water and had swallowed a lethal draught of soap suds. The full effect of this was not immediately apparent and the *ingegnere* had made an unaccustomed decision to take his horse for a ride. The combination of such an unusual event and an ultimately lethal dose of soap suds caused the horse to throw her rider. He broke his leg. This event also had a happy outcome. We bought a 2,000-litre iron cylinder, which we put in a large shaded angle behind the house to collect the rainwater off our roof, thus becoming both independent of the *ingegnere* and more ecological. Water for drinking we collected from the village fountain.

The *ingegnere* spent much time away on business. But he had installed a menage in his house consisting of his mistress, Laura, and her parents, Leonora and Leobrando. We had no contact with them. On the two occasions when we went down to tell them that the cistern was flooding, they fled indoors and did not answer our knock. Eventually, we just shouted at the top of our voices "*La cisterna e piena*" and usually they turned the pump off.

After a certain incident they became more cooperative, though not more communicative. Laura began to pace around unhappily, until one day she started to keen. Her voice was melodious, but slowly it gained in volume. Louder and louder came her plaints. About him. He had deserted her. Gave her no money. He was a bastard, a delinquent, and impotent. On and on she went and her words echoed round the valley. Slowly people began to appear on the skyline of the hill opposite. In ones and twos, then in groups, until a whole row of people stood like black dots on the ridge of the hill. She was a Medea, or Andromache, or a luckless Dejanira. This was Greek tragedy in the raw.

Laura and Leonora and Leobrando departed. The *ingegnere* was now on his own apart from his retainer, Meco. At weekends, however, many people came and went. Meanwhile, with no one living regularly in the house below, the floodings grew worse and worse until one Saturday we could stand it no longer. There was an aperture between the cistern and our main room, six feet up and closed off with a hinged, sheet iron shutter. I was encouraged to squeeze myself through this hole and "do something". And so I collected a pile of small stones and earth from outside and managed to make myself small enough to pass through. I must have been full of confidence that I could return rather than being stuck in this watery Hades. Anyway, holding my breath under water I blocked the down pipe. And with the help of a strong male guest who was staying with us, I was pulled back through the hole with much skin scraped off my shoulders, tummy, and backside.

Three hours later the *ingegnere* and Meco appeared. The *ingegnere* looked downcast and spoke rather hesitantly.

"I don't know what to do. No water is coming through and so our pump has broken. May we unscrew the down pipe outside your house?"

"Certainly!" I said.

They unscrewed the joint and poked around inside. Suddenly, a whole volley of small stones and mud came pouring out. The *ingegnere* looked at me accusingly.

"I did tell you," I said in reproof. "The wall is now so soft from the constant overflow that it is crumbling away."

He sighed. "This has been a very bad day. While my friends and I were out last night, some people from the village came and took the wheels off all our cars." And tentatively he added, "Did you hear anything?"

Wow! That was indeed a feat: wheels off at least five cars! I could scarcely restrain my laughter.

"No, we heard nothing."

Without another word he and Meco turned and trudged away. Within three months he had sold up and gone. Later we heard, what we really knew already, that he was extremely unpopular in the village. They did not like the way he treated us, nor how he treated Laura and her parents. We came to realise that village power in Italy is a force of nature.

34 Good Neighbours

We were popular in the village. Felicity spoke good Italian and they loved Carlina and Alessia, both of whom were tiny when they first came to Macina. Roger was another matter; the locals found him taciturn and enigmatic. But brave and curious souls used to come up the path and sound him out. Bit by bit he gained the reputation of being a sage. Young people came to see him to learn English, sort out mathematical problems, and talk about themselves in a way that they could not in a tight-knit community. Roger's spoken Italian was not good. His accent was very English and if he was ironic in his own language, he was pedantic in Italian. His approach to teaching English was extremely grammatical, not at all conversational. But since that was how English had traditionally been taught in Italy, his pupils thought he was a good teacher, and very wise.

His one early chum was Il Conte Bulgarini. According to Roger, Il Conte had picked him up when he was walking to the village one day.

"Come to see my castle," the Count had said in charming English.

"Ye-e-s, I would like to."

"It's my wife's castle. Come to see my wife and my son, Gheri."

"I would like to."

And so they drove to the castle, in the nearby village

of Graffignano. Stopping where the drawbridge would have been, Il Conte unlocked the gate with a huge key. They came into a large yard overgrown with weeds and enclosed by massive tall, thick walls. A number of dogs were roaming around in it. They went up a stone staircase with no handrail and a drop of twenty feet, avoiding the frequent dog mess. The stair led straight up on the left-hand side to the *piano nobile*, which had vast rooms and grey floor tiles identical to the ones in our house. Il Conte opened a door off the main room.

"This is my son, Gheri." Gheri was naked in his bath, but seemed less abashed than Roger felt.

"And here is my wife." For she had joined them at the entrance to the bathroom.

Roger had lunch there and discovered that Il Conte came from Pisa, had spent time in Brazil as a racing driver, and when the Contessa's castle became vacant they had settled in Graffignano to farm the castle land. They had two sons and a very beautiful daughter. For a time we too knew them quite well. They had lunch one day with us and we went there. Felicity was full of admiration for their marquetry furniture and old heavy carpets. Carlina was fascinated with Il Conte, particularly when he asked me outside his castle gate: "Gianni, come! Let your tyres down so that I can breathe your sweet English air!"

We came to know, rather better, a simpler family who had links with Il Conte. For one year Ugo Menichetti had farmed the land above us and he and Maria had lived in a very large *casale* attached to the land. Ugo had then retired at the age of seventy-five and they moved to a smallholding near Graffignano, which Il Conte had given them for a nominal rent. They had everything. Virgil would have approved. Beside the track that led down to the house there were caves in the soft tufa rock. Each cave was inhabited. Two large pigs in the first, white rabbits and white pigeons in the second, and a large number of hens and a stout cockerel in the third. Then the house would come into view: a simple grey stone house with an outside staircase. The large kitchen with its dusty floor was where they spent most time. But there was a shaded bower in the front where they sat in the heat of the summer. Below it lay a kitchen garden with all manner of produce: lettuces, tomatoes, runner beans, fennel, peppers and courgettes, to name but a few. An old but fruit-bearing olive tree stood in the middle. A small vineyard, impeccably tended, marched down beyond, and then a stream from which water was pumped up to service all the plants and what was needed in the house. Beyond the house was another cave. This one was hollowed out deep into the tufa. On a hot summer's day it was deliciously cool. It stored the wine, but long ago it had been a dwelling. Its temperature never varied, summer and winter, from eighteen degrees centigrade.

We used to visit them once or twice each time we went to Macina. Felicity and Maria had long conversations about rural recipes. Ugo and I talked spasmodically about weather, crops, and wine, while the children ate Maria's hard home-made bread, spread with olive oil, salt, and lightly smeared with ripe tomatoes. They lived on well into their eighties, visited by all and, latterly, helped by their numerous children.

Macina had history in its very soil. Near the spring down the hill there were the remains of a simple black and white Roman mosaic. It was clear that over the centuries the hillside had eroded and all traces of a Roman villa had disappeared. No doubt in the next 500 years our hillside would become eroded like the Badlands just to the north. On the other side of the Tiber Valley a road ran from Orvieto to Amelia. It was constructed halfway up the mountainside long ago to avoid the swamps in the valley and in the late Middle Ages a plague of malaria. When Cicero in 79BC was collecting evidence to defend his client, Roscius, from nearby Amelia, against the stooges of the dictator, Sulla, he might have ridden along this road. More definitely it was the route taken by the medieval Emperor, Frederick II, accompanied by his retinue of soldiers, Muslim clerics, monkeys, and clowns. Not much later it was thought worthwhile to build a castle beside it designed (or redesigned) by the great local architect and builder, Antonio Sangallo the Elder. But it was the Etruscans who were the first "modern" people in this region. Orvieto, known to the Romans as Urbs Vetus (the Old City) was probably the confederate centre of the Etruscan city states in Etruria, even though near Amelia their domain in this area stopped abruptly at the Tiber. The most obvious and recent historical action took place in 1944, when the Nazi army confronted the Allied troops as they moved slowly up the peninsula. Kesselring had decided to make a stand on the Badlands, taking advantage of slopes that were so treacherous for an advancing army. According to Tito, our house itself was a German machine-gun post, guarding the road as it ran over the col between the two hills. The small town of Bagnoregio, a few miles further west, took the brunt of the battle, a most unfitting event for the pious biographer of St. Francis, San Bonaventura, who had lived there. Soon afterwards, however, Orvieto was spared the damage of war by a most civilised agreement between the local German and British commanders. Despite it being an obvious strongpoint perched on its high tufa plug, the Germans left it untouched and the British did not impede their departure. In 2010 the city gave special honours to both commanders.

Sitting on the steps of Macina in the evening watching the shadows move up the Umbrian mountains beyond the Tiber Valley, one was aware of space, space in time and space of place. And if one continued to sit there after all the bats had left their holes and the chorus of night cicadas had started up, one might look up into the night and see the Milky Way unimpeded by street lights and one might count the shooting stars speeding across the black August sky. One August, when Carlina was three, she looked out of the window of her little room above the oven and the cistern and saw a dark red moon just above the mountains. Running through the bedrooms and down the stone stairs, "Mummy, why is the moon so red?" she cried. We and friends who were house guests had been talking and had not noticed. We did not know the answer to her question, but soon it became clear: a white sliver of light appeared on one edge. It was a total lunar eclipse.

On a similar occasion at a similar time of year we could imagine the American astronauts standing on the very moon we could see so well. Not that we were usually well informed about the world's events. When we were in Italy the uprising in Prague and student riots passed us by, as indeed did the day-to-day events of the Vietnam War. Instead we could look at a landscape where recorded history went back 2,700 years to the Etruscans and Oscans, whose beehive ovens and white oxen exactly mirrored images to be found on Roman sarcophagi. Having recently read Bernard Lovell's *In the Centre of Immensities*, I could look up and marvel at our galaxy with its billion stars, each probably with its own planets, and then realise that there were at least another hundred million similar galaxies – a Universe stretching back no less than 12 billion years.

We were in Rome one November and December for a sabbatical term after the end of the excavations at Lankhills. We lived in a flat belonging to the British School of Rome beside the huge main Roman market behind the Vatican. We had been alerted to the existence of this flat by my colleague and historian, gentle Peter Partner, who knew John Ward-Perkins, Bryan's father, who was the Director of the School. The lodgings were apposite, since the point of the sabbatical was to do research into Roman burial customs in order to throw light on our 500 graves in Winchester. For a time I even attended lectures on the subject at Rome University. The other point of the sabbatical was to take photographs of the varieties of architecture found in Rome to help me teach those pupils whose div don I was and who I saw for an hour every day. I remember the dark late afternoon of my thirty-fourth birthday (a day of birth that I share with the Epicurean Roman poet, Horace – not to mention the Feast of the Immaculate Conception) when by chance I was standing alone on the top of the Spanish Steps looking out towards the dome of St. Peter's, watching huge flights of autumn starlings eddying and flowing to and fro across the city. I remember thinking how old I was becoming and how much older was this ancient city.

It was in that context of time and space that a momentous thirty-fifth year started for me. It began unobtrusively as we motored back from Rome to Winchester. Felicity sat beside me in our cosy car expecting the arrival of Alessia within six weeks. Carlina was in the back seat. The Apennines were white with snow. We took a new *autostrada* that had just been built linking Lucca to Viareggio. It cut off two sides of a triangle, Lucca to Pisa and Pisa to Viareggio. It rose up in a deep valley passing through beautiful, pristine chestnut woods, and then descended towards the coast on a series of viaducts. Italians are exciting road builders, as my engineering father found out when he worked with them for two years in what was then the Gold Coast. But this road, in an unspoilt forested valley – was it really necessary? We journeyed on past Genoa, to stay a night in Alassio, where Carol and Franco had a flat. Then a night in Arles and a morning in Avignon. My mind turned back to the holiday I spent fifteen years earlier when in my first year at Oxford, Gordon Dilworth and I had stayed in Avignon for our first unparented time away from Britain. I remembered how delighted Gordon and I had been as we sat at the end of the square by the Palais des Papes and watched the fast-flowing River Rhone divided from the papal hill only by a narrow road lined with plane trees. The scene was so human. But on this later occasion that little road had become a busy, crowded dual carriageway cut into the hill on one side and embedded in the river on the other. The plane trees had disappeared and the people on bicycles had been replaced by cars.

Part 2 – FOCUSSING THE LENS

FIGHTING MOTORWAYS, 1973–1979

35 Thoughts in my Thirties

Felicity and I used to read a lot. I had to, for my teaching. Our reading did not come to a halt in Macina. The summer holidays were the time when I readied myself for those courses that depended entirely on me and not for those lessons that were followed by public examinations. In fact this was the teaching that was by far the most difficult. It required a lot of thought, including (not surprisingly) contemplation on how the world was changing. On that score what I was most conscious of was the effect of rising standards of living, especially in the West. Poorer people were being lifted out of their poverty and better housed, goods and amusements were becoming more affordable, there was greater freedom of expression, greater sexual licence, and the drug culture was becoming ingrained. This was taking place all over the West. It was also spreading, as students hitch-hiked to India through Afghanistan and jet aeroplanes made travel to the USA and Australia much easier. But I was aware, too, of the degradation of the countryside, of life lived in overcrowded cities, perhaps more lavishly but not more happily, an existence well documented by famous Italian film-makers, of the rapid rise of the global population, now around 4 billion, and the seeming depletion of natural resources. I knew of others feeling the same, and that included Felicity, although her attention was now moving towards her daughters. It was at about this time that Barbara Ward and René Dubos published their seminal book *Only One Earth: The Care and Maintenance of a Small Planet.* It made a great impression on me, for I could see it happening before my own eyes.

At all events, when after my sabbatical we arrived back in Winchester, fresh and ready to face the ordinariness of life, including the not so ordinary birth of our daughter Alessia, there was a sudden burst of activity in the town. A new motorway had been given planning permission to pass through the water meadows close to the ancient precincts of the city. A meeting of protest had been arranged. Five hundred people packed into the New Hall of Winchester College to find out how the development could be opposed.

36 The M3 through the Water Meadows
(Population – 4 billion; CO2 ppm – 330; Centigrade – + 0.7)

The motorway was not unexpected. An enquiry had been held on the route in 1970 and it had not met strong opposition. Not by Hampshire County Council, nor by Winchester City nor by Winchester College, nor by the cathedral. Routes to the west of Winchester had been opposed by Lord Rank and Lord Mountbatten through whose estates it would have passed. But in 1973 the citizens of Winchester had only just woken up. They now believed that their elected representatives with their civil servants had let them down. The recently published planning permission was obviously a *fait accompli*, except that the side roads to join the motorway still had to be decided at an inquiry. This offered just a little hope: it was possible in law, if circumstances were to change fundamentally, for protesters to oppose the main route. This was the argument used by learned barristers, John Spokes QC and Sir David Calcutt QC, in front of those 500. I was at the meeting. After my recent and not so recent thoughts it seemed right for me to oppose the motorway in whatever way I could – despite the fact that I had not opposed it earlier. The water meadows at Winchester are very beautiful, flanked as they are by the medieval buildings of St. Cross Hospital and Winchester College, with the great backbone of the Norman cathedral in behind them. People in Winchester believed that the contiguity of the meadows to the town was a unique feature. It provided the very "lungs of the city". But I decided that my reason for opposition was not that I did not like the ten lanes of the proposal so close to where I lived (though I certainly did not like them), but that no new motorways were good; traffic would always increase to fill the new lanes and as a result fill other roads. I decided that if I did not oppose something so close and so destructive, I would never act. And so I acted.

I had no idea about what I could actually achieve. But my colleague, Michael St. John Parker, who had always been keen on the workings of towns and cities, pulled me along to the meetings of a hastily formed Winchester M3 Joint Action Group held in the house of David Pare, its chairman and also both the Chairman of the Winchester Preservation Trust and the Principal of the local art college.

Its members included the chairman-to-be of the Winchester Preservation Trust, Michael Carden, Alan Weeks of the Ratepayers and Residents, Rosemary Horsey of the CPRE, and various interested private individuals like Jenny Enfield, Raymond Hitchcock, and Gordon Macpherson. Slowly plans of action were formed, and I found myself interested in the process and that such ideas as came to my mind were taken seriously. Because the UK was in the midst of a recession, there were empty shops, one of which we rented to inform people and to amass signatures to hand over to the city council. Eventually 18,000 signatures were collected. On Guy Fawkes Night that year we all joined in the city's bonfire procession leading a death's head image of the M3 to throw on to its "funeral pyre". Somehow (it was very rash of me) I found myself volunteering to raise money; the Scot in me had been appalled that there had been no appeal at the New Hall meeting. We put an advertisement into the *Hampshire Chronicle* for a paid fundraiser and I found myself employing Brigadier Bobby Guinness, RE, a contemporary of my father in the Sappers. He came to work in the little watch mender's shop that had lain vacant beside the well-known pub, the Wykeham Arms. Bobby worked very hard for eighteen months and raised £9,000 net, no mean feat at that time.

Gradually I found myself becoming an intermediary. I represented the College (*faut de mieux*) at the M3JAG meetings. And I had the support of Lord Aldington, a Wykehamist friend of the prime minister, Ted Heath. Aldington at this stage did not want to be too obviously involved. But for me there was a party political involvement. I was encouraged by Jenny Enfield to join the Conservative Party and be a member of the Macleod Society, so called after Iain Macleod, the left-leaning Tory Chancellor cut short recently in his prime. Part of the point of joining was to make the strong local Conservative Association and the city council oppose the road. This eventually led to an attempt to deselect the Conservative MP, Rear Admiral Morgan Giles, who favoured the motorway. A proposition to this effect was put forward at a large meeting in the Guildhall. We knew that we had a lot of support in the city itself; and several colleagues from Winchester College, like Richard Bass and Johnny Stow, were involved. Before the meeting started these supporters all came into the main hall of the Guildhall; there must have been over 300. But minutes before the scheduled start, bus after bus drew up outside the building and disgorged rural supporter of the MP after rural supporter. The Guildhall was stuffed full, and the proposition was defeated by some 700 votes to 300.

The side-roads inquiry was eventually set for June 1976. Now we had to raise money. That February I met Lord Aldington in his office at Grindley's Bank. The office was in a high-rise building in the City of London. Through the large plate-glass windows I could see the Thames in the early spring sunshine and further off the Houses of Parliament. Lord Aldington was a man of considerable charm who, to judge by the photographs round the room, had many friends across the world from France to Saudi Arabia to Japan and Australia. He gave me the vital signal to raise money from Old Wykehamists. All the Old Wykehamists were contacted; 40 per cent replied, mostly with ten-pound notes, and £21,000 was raised to pay for a planning barrister, David Keene, who had represented the College on some other occasions. That was the result of the first trawl; then we had another when it was needed, which resulted in a further £13,000.

Meanwhile another contact had been made. This time with John Tyme. He was a virulent opponent of motorways for the same reason as I was. But his wife had been killed on one, which lent his opposition a particular force. He was a lecturer in Environmental Studies at Sheffield Polytechnic. At all events, he had already roused people not only to oppose new fast roads, but to prevent inquiries actually opening. With this gambit he had had considerable success in the Aire Valley in his native Yorkshire. The M3 Joint Action Group decided to invite him to Winchester. The meeting took place in our large living room. Large? Because by this time I was a housemaster of a boarding house at the College. There were about twenty people present, including cautious solicitors and other professional people. John spoke passionately to the effect that the only way to stop the motorway was to prevent the side-roads inquiry from opening, so that its remit could be changed to enable a challenge to the very existence of the proposed road on the grounds that the oil crisis of the time had changed circumstances – fundamentally; and so, we needed to make such a noise that the inspector in opening the inquiry could not be heard. To my surprise everybody agreed that this was the way forward, but at the same time we should have barristers present to deal with other eventualities. As a result Terence Morris, the Professor of Criminology at LSE, and I volunteered to see John Tyme in action, opposing the construction of the M25 at Hornchurch in April 1976. On that occasion he was impressive, but not successful. The crowd was not large enough.

So the scene was set. But one matter was not quite in place. David Keene, the barrister now representing both the Action Group and Winchester College, could not be present for the first three days of the inquiry. Michael Howard, who was also a planning barrister and had a house in Abbots Worthy just up the Itchen Valley from Winchester, offered to take his place. David Pare and I went up to his chambers in London to instruct him.

In the meantime, John Tyme made sure that all the television networks knew what was about to happen. There was even going to be a documentary made, by Granada TV's *World in Action*. To my amusement and some apprehension the producer of that documentary wanted to focus on me. "You're in the very nerve centre of the action," he explained. "You are the link between Winchester College and the Joint Action Group, the link between the barristers and John Tyme, and you are also the main fundraiser." I took advice from friends and decided that I should take that role. And so, before the inquiry Granada Television interviewed me with Terence Morris on camera in the War Cloisters at the College and I played a lead part in a televised meeting of the Joint Action Group with John Tyme in the house of Raymond and Joyce Hitchcock.

37 The M3 Inquiry

Following a dry winter and spring, the summer of 1976 was extremely hot. Trees died and the smaller chalk streams of Hampshire disappeared. In our large garden a huge holm oak, at least 300 years old collapsed and our extensive lawn was brown and baked. We kept flowers and vegetables alive only by siphoning bath water out of the window. The end of June was especially hot. The inquiry opened on a scorching, sun-blasted day with the thermometer showing 33 degrees C. The Winchester Guildhall was packed; with over a thousand people present there was standing room only. The lights for the television cameras only increased the heat, and the MP for Winchester, Rear Admiral Morgan Giles, sweated for all to see in the gallery.

Actually the inquiry did not open. As soon as the inspector came in, he was greeted with a huge and prolonged roar, catcalls, and the stamping of feet. This continued for some twenty minutes. I cannot remember all the details, but the inquiry was adjourned to the next day. The next day the same thing happened; there were shouts and whistles and the police dragged the noisiest people, at random, out of the hall; and the temperature crept up to 34 degrees C. Again the inquiry was adjourned. On the third day the inspector allowed people to speak without opening the inquiry. People did speak. Their tone was polite and in complete contrast to the mayhem of the previous days. Especially impressive were the words of the Mayor of Winchester, Barbara Carpenter-Turner. The inquiry was now adjourned for four weeks because the Guildhall had been booked for only three days. This allowed time for reflection, and for David Keene to take over as our barrister. Poor Michael Howard! He had sat there looking more and more thunderous and no doubt becoming more and more determined to represent "the party of law and order". As for me, an odd thing had happened. I was sitting behind Michael along with Giles Clarke who was training to be a barrister and taking meticulous notes. I was keeping out of the way, ready to step in if needed. In the midst of a particularly noisy spell along came a representative of Granada: "We want you to leave the meeting in protest, shouting as you go!"

"Sorry, but that is not my role; I have to be ready to keep the whole thing going."

"No, you must go!"

"No, I won't!" And I didn't. I was not an actor in a television drama. The other person for whom I felt sorry was the poor inspector, Major General Edge, late of the Royal Engineers and the Ordnance Survey. He was clearly a very decent and able person and was trying to bring the meeting to order, but by the end of the third day he was shaking and looked exhausted.

In the last week of July, with the temperature still close to 30 degrees C, the inquiry "began" again, but this time in the John Stripe Theatre at the teacher training college, King Alfred's. The auditorium could only hold 300. Perhaps the promoters of the motorway, the Department of Transport, hoped that 300 would be a more manageable number. It was not. Again the noise was deafening. But this time there was a new tactic: many people brought in newspapers (the *Daily Telegraph* was particularly favoured) and then, hiding behind them, proceeded to sing at the top of their voices "Rule Britannia", "Jerusalem", and "Land of Hope and Glory"! It was a most comic scene. The stewards, courteous to the end, would draw a newspaper to one side and ask "Are you singing, Madam?" "Oh no, no, no!" would come the answer. On the second day in this new venue events seemed to be coming to a climax. The inspector looked more and more desperate and had called in the police to eject protestors. Intuitively, rightly or wrongly, I decided to take part. I was holding a great sheaf of books and notes which I thought were important. And so, I handed them to John Thorn, the headmaster of Winchester College, who was now on holiday, and asked him to look after them; I was going to have myself chucked out. John took the bundle, looking rather bemused. Out I went with a huge shout, probably abusive, and was immediately put into a half nelson by a very large policeman who hauled me out through a side door. Feeling somewhat sore, I made my way round to the foyer in the front, and, just as I entered, I saw John coming out through the auditorium door. He too had shouted something, as I was told, and had been escorted out, turning round and exclaiming again "I'll be back!" That was the turning point. The inquiry was once again adjourned, and later that day it was announced that the inquiry would no longer be into the side roads but would examine once again, after a long adjournment, the main route and the need for it. We had won the first round.

The inquiry did not start again for a long time, partly because General Edge had developed an incapacitating problem with his fingers, which prevented him from writing. Whatever the problem was, it was surely the result of severe stress. But he did come back. And then the inquiry meandered on and on, well into 1977. The M3 Joint Action Group and others argued for an upgraded six-lane bypass, instead of a six-lane motorway flanked by the original four-lane by-pass. Finally, and quickly, in 1979 General Edge produced his report: the motorway was to reach the edge of Winchester, but not go through the water meadows; they were too precious in their relationship to the city and there was a chance that the water-table would be lowered. That in turn could rot the wooden piles on which the three major medieval buildings were founded: the cathedral, the Hospice of St. Cross, and Winchester College.

That, of course, was not the end of it. There had to be another inquiry to establish where the M3 could go, if not through the water meadows.

38 Postscript to the M3 Inquiry

My last little encounter with the M3 took place in 1980 after Mrs. Thatcher's new Conservative government had been elected. There was a small problem. The map in

General Edge's report showed the end of the M3 curling menacingly towards the water meadows. Would that route be taken after all, despite what General Edge wrote in print? To nip that possibility in the bud three of us went up to Westminster to explain our fears, and to say that the map seemed to preclude the possibility of putting the motorway through a tunnel under St. Catherine's Hill. Norman Fowler was the Secretary of State for the Environment and under him was the Minister of Transport, Kenneth Clarke. At our meeting with them they were courteous and listened. "The motorway will not go through the water meadows." But the politicians were not to be drawn on what it would do.

In the event the decision of the next inquiry in 1988 was that it would go through Twyford Down, but in a cutting not a tunnel. That in turn led to all sorts of demonstrations. The tunnel was apparently too expensive. Whether it was much more expensive than the measures to keep the public both under control and happy was another matter. Since then major trunk roads like the A27 round Brighton have been happily put into tunnels.

As for the 1976 inquiry, there were casualties – quite apart from the inspector's fingers and well-being. Michael Howard was not selected to be the next Conservative candidate for the Winchester Constituency. That prize went to the suave John Browne, a matinee idol but not much else. John Thorn, after he retired at the age of sixty from Winchester College, had difficulty finding a job that matched his considerable abilities. David Keene, on the other hand, pursued a successful career at the bar becoming Sir David Keene, a High Court Judge, a Privy Councillor, and a close friend of the Blairs; his time at Winchester is never mentioned.

THE BOARDING HOUSE – MOBERLY'S, 1975–1982

39 Being a Housemaster

Two years before the M3 Inquiry John Thorn asked me to be the housemaster at Moberly's, a boys' boarding house at Winchester College. This was promotion and I accepted, not without reservations. John was, it seemed, aware of them. "You may find it incarcerating. Not like the political world you have begun to inhabit." I had, however, already experienced incarceration at Groton and St. Andrew's. I had been a "dormitory" master at both schools and main carer for anything up to thirty boys. But Moberly's was inhabited by fifty-seven, and the housemaster and his wife had a staff of eight who not only kept the place spick and span, but also provided all the meals. A Winchester College house aimed to be a family. This meant that Felicity had a considerable part to play; she too had reservations.

We moved into the house in August 1975. Carlina and Alessia were thrilled, particularly Carlina who had long entertained a fantasy of living in such a grand house. There was a huge garden, a rose garden which the previous housemaster's wife, Margaret Kettle, had nurtured, and a walled vegetable garden and orchard that was home to no fewer than seventeen varieties of fruit, including a very old and prolific mulberry tree. It was a magical place. And the house too was magical. It was Elizabethan. Both girls had panelled bedrooms: Carlina's was painted white and Alessia's was brown oak. Beyond the private accommodation were passages, dormitories, and rooms of all descriptions to explore. At the very end lived Miriam Hart, the matron. Carlina and Alessia, now seven and two years old, soon learned that here was another grown-up friend with whom to chat, pass the time, and help.

The public rooms on the private side were impressive. The big, square Georgian front door led through an anteroom into the hallway which was panelled, some of it dating back four centuries. There was a wine cellar off it, which in Elizabethan times was the front door with an imposing double entry, the lintels and central pillar of which could still be seen. The large drawing room on the *piano nobile* (above an equally large study) had been refashioned in Victorian times. It was full of light and well proportioned, with white panelling on both sides of its welcoming fireplace. Its huge window faced due west and overlooked the lawn. Felicity took great pride in decorating and furnishing it. Our bedroom next door with a large bathroom en suite was wonderfully sunny in the evening. We basked in its light during the summery August before the boys arrived at the beginning of the school year. Being a housemaster was hard work. Up at seven to welcome the cook, and bed after midnight. I am a reasonably early riser, but prefer not to go to bed in the small hours of the morning. Perhaps I need not have done it; some housemasters did not. But my view was that teenagers need their sleep, and it was best for them, if they were still up without my permission, that they knew I might come round.

The boys were very varied in their talents: musical composers and performers, games players, artists, carpenters, and actors/producers. Two enormously diligent, caring, and interesting house tutors helped to foster these accomplishments, expand their academic interests, and encourage those who were not so talented. They did not live in the house, but came in most evenings. Miriam Hart lived in; her personality and presence were vital.

My position as a father substitute was a difficult act for almost sixty boys. In the past Winchester boarding houses seldom contained more than forty. Financial pressures meant that the number slowly rose to fifty, then to sixty, or even seventy. Too much in my opinion, especially as the housemaster had ultimate responsibility for the housekeeping (done in our case by Felicity) and the domestic and kitchen staff, not to mention two little girls. There were frequent attempts by the Bursary to introduce central feeding on the grounds of cost. But the system never changed for reasons of tradition if nothing else, and because housemasters tended to become possessive of their domains. After I retired there was a change. The maximum stay for housemasters reduced from fifteen years to ten to prevent them becoming burnt out.

An important aspect of the position was that the housemaster decided which boys did or did not come to his house. This provided a good start to the relationship between him and the parents with whom he dealt; for the parents were the arbiters of which housemaster and house they thought best for their child. I experienced an important test of that. One fifteen-year-old asked me if he could accept an invitation to lunch from John Smyth, the evangelical barrister and friend of Mary Whitehouse. I had developed a distrust of evangelicals at Oxford because their sense of sin tended to make them "prey" on vulnerable people, and when those vulnerable people tried to leave their coterie they were subject to a barrage of emotional blackmail. As Smyth's invitation would take the boy some five miles by bicycle out of Winchester and away from the college's jurisdiction, I said "No! Sorry!" Not unnaturally the boy was indignant and persuaded his parents to intervene. They came to the house and we talked over the matter with a cup of tea. I explained why I had said "No!", and they must have had enough confidence in my judgement to agree with it. Thirty-five years later John Smyth's practices on such occasions were widely reported. The "boy" now in his fifties sent me a charming email thanking me for "having been right".

Difficulties, however, could occur when housemasters changed. The boys in the middle of the house, and their parents too, might not like the newcomer. This is where I had difficulties, because these boys, in the middle of their teens, were likely anyway to be the most rebellious. The older boys were enormously helpful and friendly when I first became their housemaster. And that was the case again three or four years on. We were pleased when they seemed to be at home on the private side. But we did make the rule that they could not just drop in on our drawing room, because our bedrooms were on the same floor.

On the whole the boys were very good with each other. The old prefect system, with its possibilities of corruption, had mostly disappeared. This could have meant that the senior boys no longer cared, but care they did for the younger boys' welfare. The possibility of bullying worried me, and was what I asked the prefects to be particularly vigilant about. It did sometimes occur in a psychological, not physical form. This seemed to me to be more important than the problems of smoking and drinking which mainly occurred in the town because it was so close. Drugs, however, were another matter, though I believe I was not very good at pursuing the clues.

40 Ghosts in an Old House

During our time in the house my view of reality was widened in rather unusual directions. Some years before, in my first spring term in Winchester, I was watching that form of football which is peculiar to the school. I was joined by Mr. Jackson, who wanted to explain the extraordinary niceties of this game. Mr. Jackson, normally known as The Jacker, had been housemaster of Moberly's between the wars and up to 1946. He was a schoolmaster of the very old type. He went around in baggy brown trousers and a baggy brown jacket, and often wore a shapeless, baggy brown raincoat. The story goes that two Wykehamists were in the town at a time and place that were not allowed. They saw The Jacker not far behind them, and bearing down. Luckily they also saw a policeman close by: "Please, Sir," they said to the policeman (Wykehamists are on the whole very polite). "We're being followed by a dirty old man." The policeman in turn bore down on The Jacker. History does not relate what passed between them. Whatever it was it gave the boys time to make good their escape.

Now it was The Jacker who told me about the ghost while we were watching this game. "Do you know about the ghost in Moberly's, Macdonald?" (He knew that I was a tutor in the house at the time.)

"No! Is there one?"

"Oh yes! He is a Jacobean gentleman, dressed all in black with a white ruff."

"What does he do?"

"He walks about on his knees, because the Victorians took the floors up two feet."

"Can you see the feet from below?"

"I never have. I have always met him upstairs."

"Does he then disappear?"

"No. Not always. He has been known to sit at the end of a visitor's bed."

At that point something, apparently very interesting, happened on the football field, and The Jacker changed the subject to teach me more about this interesting game.

When I took the house over from Kenneth Kettle, Kenneth warned me about the ghost. He had not experienced it himself, but Miriam had, and so, I asked her about it. Miriam was a shy person, but charmingly straightforward. She told me that she was in the Elizabethan gallery above the drawing room. The boys' laundry was kept in cupboards there. One Easter holiday, just before the start of the summer term, she was sorting out the sheets. She heard Kenneth coming up the wooden stairs. And the door swung open. Kenneth was nowhere to be seen. This happened two or three times. She became used to it and assumed it was a ghost.

When we arrived in the house, there was no sign of the ghost. But one Saturday in October 1978, an event did occur. It happened on Hallowe'en. Even more banal, it happened after we returned from a party where we had been asked to dress as ghosts or witches. And of course there was a full moon. At twenty-past two I was woken up by a vivid flash. A mirror had fallen off the wall and had reflected the bright light of the full moon into my eyes. Simultaneously I heard the sound of running feet in the gallery above. Thinking that the boys were having a Hallowe'en party, I ran up the stairs knowing that I could cut them off before they could get back to their dormitories. Upstairs there was no one.

I went down again. Then I heard a sound, a rushing, mighty sound of water, somewhere on the ground floor. I investigated and heard the sound coming from an old, very dusty lavatory that had not been used since the time of Len, an ancient retainer who had died a year previously. In this lavatory I saw both taps in the hand basin were pouring out water full pelt. I could not turn them off; they were jammed. And so I went to fetch a monkey wrench. That did the job. But on coming out of the dusty lavatory, I noticed my dusty footprints on the highly polished linoleum on the passage floor. There were no other footprints. Why were there no other footprints? Would that not mean that nobody else had entered the lavatory? And that somehow the taps had turned themselves on? Was this the work of the "ghost"?

I soon found out. There were living in the attic at the time, near the Elizabethan gallery, an alternative couple, Sandy and Alfie, who looked after the huge kitchen garden in return for lodging. They had been away over the Hallowe'en weekend. But every night after their return, between midnight and one o'clock, they were woken by the most almighty crash somewhere in the attic, possibly in the gallery. We heard it too, less loudly. This went on for a fortnight. Sandy and Alfie were becoming most upset, quite apart from being deprived of their sleep. So, I decided that I had to do something.

I went to the school chaplain, Paul Bates.

"Paul, are you any good at bell, book, and candle?"

"No, not really. What's the problem?"

I told him the whole story starting with The Jacker. He listened very carefully.

"Look, Jock. The ghost has inhabited the house far longer than you. Perhaps he is afraid that you are going to evict him. Why not just leave him? He'll probably calm down."

And so we did. And he did. Nothing more happened. It was, however, interesting that our ghostly visitations did take place at a time when other curious events were happening nearby. My colleague, John Durran, owned a house in Canon Street just along the road from us. His tenant, a young woman, was being terrified by teapots flying through the air. At least, that was the story. But Canon Street had once been a notorious, narrow little street full of pubs, brothels and curious goings-on. It was not a very long time previously that boys living in boarding houses further up the hill were not allowed to walk down that street on their way to lessons. At the top of the street is a seventeenth-century house called the Queen's Lodge, lived in at that time by a woman called Hecate Boyle. Since Hecate was the Queen of the Witches and of the Moon, it was not surprising that this mortal Hecate took part in regular séances. These occurred in the house at the bottom of Canon Street belonging to Belle Gaunt, the wife of Canon Gaunt, once a don at Winchester College. Years later I discovered that the latter house was also haunted. Our friends, the Parry-Jones, had to have the presence exorcised, or more precisely "re-buried". The reburial was successful, even though in religious matters our friends were confirmed agnostics.

But the history of the ghost in Moberly's did take another turn. Some two years after we left the house, I happened to visit our successors, James and Ruth Miller. I had never told them about the ghost, because I thought James would just scoff, and I had kept away up to that time so as not to cramp their style. They welcomed me very warmly indeed, and I soon discovered why. "Is this house haunted?" Ruth asked. Apparently, her sister who had just departed after a visit was very sensitive to such matters and had declared that she never wanted to come and stay again; she did not like the feel of the house. And so, I told them the story of our experience, leaving out what The Jacker had told me.

Some months later I visited James and Ruth again. Again they were pleased to see me. "Do you know what?" Ruth exclaimed. "My sister, hearing that the house is haunted, decided that she ought to pluck up the courage to stay again. And… she actually saw the ghost. He was sitting at the end of her bed. He was a Jacobean man in a black doublet and hose. Isn't that amazing?" It certainly was amazing, because I had never told them The Jacker's stories about the visitations and the Jacobean gentleman. Many years later, long after the Millers had left the College, I met them again at a party. And just to make sure, I asked Ruth in James' hearing if she remembered the incident of her sister with the Jacobean gentleman. She certainly had, she said. But it was obvious that James, a very dedicated Oxford economist by training, was not interested.

41 The Ancient Art (or Science?) of Astrology

Towards the end of our time in Moberly's I became interested in astrology. There were three reasons for this odd behaviour. First, in my reading of the Roman historians, Tacitus and Suetonius, I could not help but notice that the early Roman Emperors were constantly exiling or otherwise punishing astrologers. Second, any student of English literature and the Middle Ages knows that Chaucer often refers to astrological matters, for instance in the characterisation of the Wyf of Bath who had numerous husbands or in the charming farmyard tale of Chauntecleer and Pertelote. The famous medieval churches of Chartres and Vezelay also have whole chapels adorned with signs of the zodiac. Finally, in the New Age thinking of the 1970s, astrology became popular. Even the new American President, Ronald Reagan, was influenced by it. In Britain the prolific composer, Michael Tippett, wrote *Moving into the Age of Aquarius,* based on the astrological view that there are Great Years lasting two millennia each; the planet is now coming out of the Great Year of Pisces and going into the Great Year of Aquarius, which according to astrologers will be a time of huge change. Encouraged by a couple of friends I had my chart read by Rachel Jessel, who I had never met before.

The chart described the person I am and the sort of situations I find myself in. As a character study and more it was extremely accurate, not only by my reckoning but by that of others. I decided to look further into the matter. I bought Derek and Julia Parker's book, which enabled me to cast the horoscopes of other people, with their permission. These readings are not the simple horoscopes you see in popular newspapers and magazines. Up to fifty different variables have to be taken into account and each variable be given a different weight. For instance the sign of the Ascendant is much more important than the astrological nature of the planet Neptune. The skill of an astrologer is not unlike that of an historian who has to weigh up the value of each source of information. For me, much depended on the dependability of the 1979 edition of the Parkers' guide.

Certainly, my results were hardly worse than Rachel's. My victims were impressed by their accuracy. To make quite sure that I was not influenced by my knowledge of them I carried out an experiment. Three friends each chose a person I did not know and gave me their date, time, and place of birth. I wrote out three charts, without any reference to the basic astrology. The three people then had to choose the chart that each thought was his or her own. Each chose correctly. On another occasion I offered a reading as a raffle prize at an official dinner. A woman I did not know won it; I warned her that it could be revealing. It was. Her comment was "You know much more about me than anyone else I know!" And that included her husband. Luckily I have a bad memory. Twins could be a problem. I have only once cast the horoscope of twins. Recently my wife's god-daughter and niece gave birth to identical girl twins twenty minutes apart. Within that twenty minutes, the Ascendant changed from Gemini to Cancer. Though the girls are identical to look at, their characters are very different.

And so, what is my verdict on this "superstition"? Since it works with an impressive accuracy, it is not a superstition. Why it works, I can only guess. It has been in the human psyche for at least 5,000 years, and in all likelihood for much longer. Perhaps that is a cause. I suspect that the actual stars and planets do not have an influence. But their positions in relation to celestial constellations and to the temporal and local position of each person are analogous to what is posited in chaos theory. We are all linked to everything else. For millennia, planets and constellations have been the most obvious markers of time and space. With computers gaining power in a steep, geometric progression, perhaps they will give an answer. Professor Brian Cox, the popular TV physicist and space expert, has called astrology a superstition. He was wrong about that. But the question is: how useful is it?

Casting a horoscope is a complex and time-consuming business. It is far too slow for the practicalities of our modern world. It could easily become an obsession. Sometimes it can be useful, for instance in helping someone with psychological problems. It can also be dangerous if a person thinks that her or his way of thinking is fixed and cannot be modified. I have no view about predicting the future. That is a much more complex matter, although a knowledge of someone's character and the space that he or she occupies obviously gives some evidence about that person's future. I am not surprised that the early Roman Emperors took the science so seriously. If an astrologer was able to get hold of the place, date, and time of an emperor's birth, he would know much about that emperor's inner workings. Not something that a Caligula or Domitian would have wanted to become common knowledge. And astrologers were also thought to be able to say when an emperor's death was due. That could play havoc with would-be aspirants. The science was so abstruse and so dependent on mathematics that its practitioners were called "mathematici". The clever, later emperor, Hadrian, however, used it for his own benefit. What about people today with power and responsibility? Nancy and Ronald Reagan used astrology. And Ronald Reagan was not a bad president of the USA.

42 Dreams

At the beginning of the spring holidays before my last term in Moberly's I had a very vivid dream. I was on the Isle of Skye under the Red Cuillin mountains on the Broadford Road, and I could see the buffers at the end of the railway tracks at Kyle of Lochalsh over the sea on the mainland. I had just alighted from a bubble car when I saw a skirt belonging to my mother lying on the ground. At that moment a posse of soldiers with my father in command came marching past. I looked up the nearest mountain and saw yew trees growing up its side. The mountain was in shadow until the last hundred feet or so, which were bathed in sunlight. I decided to climb up to that sunny peak. Just into the sunshine I found a party in progress under a trellis of vines. Some of the party were standing; others were lounging on couches. "Oh!" they exclaimed. "You're early!" I looked back down the path and saw a woman tightly wrapped around in something that resembled a dark cloak, which was pulled over her head. Then I woke up.

At lunchtime I was telephoned by my sister. "I'm very sorry, Jock, but I have to tell you… Mum died this morning at about midday…"

The dream gave me comfort. In a sense I had been there with her. She was nearly eighty-one. She had suffered a minor heart attack three years earlier, but she had recovered well and there was no sign of an imminent death. A few months earlier my parents had returned from Herefordshire, where they had been living near my sister, to be in their home city of Edinburgh. Joan Mary was staying with them the day she died. They had gone for a stroll beside Blackford Pond – one of my mother's favourite haunts. She had sat down on a bench to watch the ducks while my father and Joan Mary walked on. When they walked back, she was dead. She could not have had it easier: her daughter was there, she loved the place, and had died at a decent age. As for me, I was there too. Every single detail in my dream was symbolically accurate.

POLITICAL ACTION in WINCHESTER, 1982–1994

43 A Local Election

John Thorn was right. I did feel somewhat incarcerated as a housemaster. I had begun to consider my next step. I toyed with the idea of becoming a headmaster, of a day school. I was put on the long list for the headship of Kings College School, Wimbledon, where there had been a bust-up between the head and the Bursar. I had one interview but did not proceed further. Sir David Calcutt was a person I knew quite well. We had met while we were both fighting the M3 Motorway, and he had become a Fellow of Winchester College; that is, he was a Governor. "Why don't you become a barrister?" he asked. "You would be a good barrister. I have been thinking about it. It would be good for my chamber to have some fresh air, someone who has not been in law the whole time, a person who could do half his time in chambers and half elsewhere – in your case at Winchester College. What about it? You could do it!"

I was intrigued and tempted. I had been told that it was more difficult to find a place in a chamber than to pass the relevant exams. I counted up my funds. They could cover much of the apprenticeship period. But then I would be exposed to a six-month gap. With a family, I could not do it. I did not try to become a barrister.

In March 1981 the SDP was formed by the Gang of Four. Roy Jenkins, Shirley Williams, David Owen, and Bill Rodgers had split away from the internal quarrels of the Labour Party. This, I thought, was more my scene. I had become increasingly interested in politics. The late seventies had witnessed great problems of inflation, social disorder and unrest. I had read *Small is Beautiful* by E. F. Schumacher, and then *Enough is Enough* by John Taylor. He was Bishop of Winchester, and a very saintly man. I knew him a little and liked him a lot. He was very worried by the country's increasing materialism. Industrial unrest was the more obvious problem. And so partly for that reason I had voted for Mrs. Thatcher's Conservative Party in 1979. But I had voted for her also because she was a scientist with a Chemistry degree from Oxford. She would be more aware of green issues, once immediate problems had been faced. I thought too that a woman prime minister would bring about a new approach. It was not until 1988 that she did start looking at a green policy with her then ambassador to the UN, Sir Crispin Tickell.

She did not embark on that course quickly enough for me. Consequently, with somebody whose name to my shame I cannot remember I helped in 1980 to start up the Green Party (then called the Ecology Party) in Winchester. We were not obtrusive, but we did ask Jonathon Porritt, the main leader of the Ecology Party, to speak to a group of about twenty in our drawing room. He spoke well, but did not convince his audience. The adversarial structure of British politics then, as now, made it very difficult for a new party to get off the ground. Since then, however, Jonathon

Porritt has become a by-word for stamina, resilience, and for his huge knowledge and support for environmental sustainability. Nevertheless, back in 1980 in Winchester we did start bottle banks and we did do a count of commuters in polluting cars that held only the driver. In a period of three hours during the morning rush hour we found that 92 per cent of cars contained only the driver. With the world's population now moving past 4.5 billion and the carbon content in the atmosphere also moving up, Felicity and I decided not to enlarge our family any further.

Then the SDP was formed. The Liberals pressed me to join them. But I joined the SDP on its very first day. I thought that in an alliance with the green-leaning Liberals I could help develop a "green DNA" in the SDP. I signed up as a member in the Winchester constituency steering group that had been formed, and then chaired, by Dr. Whitfield, a GP who lived in Micheldever. I volunteered to stand for Winchester City Council in the spring, gave John Thorn my notice as a housemaster, and went up to London to be vetted as a potential parliamentary candidate. After I had passed muster, the standing committee in Winchester apportioned out SDP members for council wards. Dr. Whitfield was very keen that I should contest the ward that contained two small villages near Winchester, Crawley and Sparsholt. He thought that I had the right voice and credentials to woo one of the most Conservative wards in the district.

I was lucky. The ward was small: only these two villages and two or three small hamlets. There was a large Tory majority over Labour. But the Conservative county council wanted to cancel the school bus to and from Sparsholt. The village, apparently, was 150 yards too close to Winchester. Everybody would now have to walk the three miles (minus

150 yards) or go by car to Winchester along the single lane, steep-banked rural road. Though this was strictly the concern of the county council and not the city council, it fitted exactly my green agenda.

I heard through Peter Partner that a friend of his, June Bennett, who lived in Sparsholt had told him that there was going to be a meeting in the village hall. And so I went to it on a freezing February night. Though unknown to most people I launched into a passionate speech: "Think of all those unnecessary car journeys, all those petrol fumes, think of the danger to children walking along that road in the dark and cars passing them one after the other!" I finished by announcing my candidacy for the city elections. After the meeting I joined several people pacing out the distance all the way to Winchester and its closest secondary school.

My mother's funeral in Edinburgh took place soon after, but the sun shone for the rest of the spring holidays. For the first afternoon of canvassing I went out on my bicycle. Straightaway I found supporters, people who approved of my bicycle. From then on I canvassed very hard, sensing I could win. But I cheated somewhat. Bicycling from Winchester to Sparsholt and even further to Crawley was not a good use of my limited time. I soon took to loading the bicycle into the car and parking near the entry to each village. Then I was ready to canvas. I was much helped by new allies in each village who delivered leaflets and on election day sat "telling" outside the two polling stations. The turn-out was very large for a local election. Before my supporters and I went to the count at the Guildhall, it was clear that we really might win.

In the end my winning margin was thirty-five votes, despite the fact that the Conservatives had received a huge boost in the opinion polls because of the Falklands War.

The sitting councillor was not pleased. She thought that I had won unfairly, using a county council matter to promote myself into the city council. Someone described my win as an "Exocet". Unfortunately the Exocet did not hole Mrs. Thatcher's ship below the waterline.

44. Parliamentary Elections, 1983 and 1987

(Population – 5 billion; CO2 ppm – 350; Centigrade – +0.8)

Four Liberals and I sat together in alliance on Winchester City Council. I was the only SDP councillor to win in Hampshire. There were also five Labour members and forty-three Conservatives. The five in the Alliance was at least an increase on the two Liberals the previous year. Coming back into politics was John Matthew, the Under Bursar at Winchester College. He had stood for Parliament as a Liberal in the seventies. His early career as a District Commissioner in the Colonial Office meant that soon after this election he was flown to the Falklands to help in their recovery from the war.

It took me some time to find my feet, much assisted though I was by my Liberal colleagues. But the council officers were also very helpful, as were some left-leaning Conservatives and a right-leaning Labour member. I was on the Planning Committee, where I surprised officers and members alike by inspecting the sites of planning applications in wards other than my own. I was also on the Housing Committee, where extraordinarily restrictive rules were most frustrating, rules laid down by government to help the Right to Buy and prevent the building of new council houses. One did not have to be a clairvoyant to sense trouble in the future.

The twelve years I spent on Winchester City Council were in many ways very satisfying. The year I left, 1994, saw the Liberal Democrats (the name for the now amalgamated Liberals and SDP) take control with twenty-eight councillors. In two of those years I stood for Parliament. In 1983 I did not stand much of a chance. But my colleagues and I had fun. I enjoyed finding out about the constituency, visiting businesses, schools, and farms and trying out a green tinge to the central SDP manifesto. My agent was John Matthew's son, David. He was at university and knew more about elections than I did. He found a constituency office for us in the high street, above a shoe shop. Two architects shared the same floor. They took great delight in teasing us by peering round the door and whispering "Mrs. Thatcher…" in melancholy tones. I enjoyed too the count on the night of the election. The Returning Officer was the High Sheriff of Hampshire who had laid a massive bet on John Browne being re-elected. But it so happened that my votes were being counted more quickly than his. At one point I was ahead by 15,000 to his 11,000. The High Sheriff was becoming more and more agitated and was consoling himself with stiff whiskies. But the lead did not last and the pallor on his face became a healthy flush. The Alliance in Winchester did not do too badly. We won 33 per cent of the votes, up from less than 20 per cent for the Liberals in 1979.

The 1987 General Election was a different matter. Everybody thought that in Winchester we had a chance. John Browne and his wife were in the throes of a divorce. He was suing her for not dividing with him her very healthy inheritance, which was thought to be in a bank in Jersey. She was prepared to go to prison rather than give in to him. The local Conservatives did not approve of a man who was happy to send his wife to jail. I stayed out of the whole matter, but

Elizabeth Browne kept on phoning me, dishing out the dirt on her estranged husband. So much so that I was almost sorry for him, and when it came to casting my own vote the pencil hovered tantalisingly over the space beside John Browne.

In this election I came to appreciate the traps laid for parliamentary candidates. In two very different pubs, one a famous pub in Winchester and another almost as famous in a village, I felt a hand groping my testicles from behind. Turning round all I could see were the innocent and smiling faces of women. More serious were the efforts of pharmaceutical companies to gain my support. There was one company of which I should perhaps have been more wary. But only "perhaps". An executive of a Dutch tunnelling and dredging firm wanted to support the SDP for its pro-European policies. And so he took a party of friends including me to examine the new and exciting Scheldt Dam project. We arrived in Rotterdam airport and went immediately to the Scheldt estuary. On a bright, breezy June day on the North Sea, we boarded a sturdy tug to ride the buffeting waves all along the dam to see how it worked. After that came a very pleasant evening in a peaceful, rural hostelry. My campaign funds were improved by £1,000.

I made a bad strategic mistake in my campaign. I estimated that I could count on the support of a majority in Winchester itself, and so I concentrated my own canvassing on the villages outside. The response in the village of Bentworth was symbolic. A friend and I had come to the end of a mostly abortive sweep when I went up to the last house. A fierce looking collie mongrel barred my path. Looking steadfastly into its eyes I reached the front door, knocked, and when my knock was not answered, delivered a leaflet. Then I backed away with the dog firmly in my sights.

Reaching the middle of the public road I turned round, and immediately it bit me in the calf. First aid was the priority in the next village where I was due to speak to a gathering (very small in the event) in the village hall. But worse was to come at the count. Soon after the polls had closed, the ballot box for Bentworth was opened before any others. I was standing by the box in the normal way to gauge the amount of support the Alliance had in Bentworth before its votes were transferred to the common piles. I counted assiduously but not one person in Bentworth voted for me. A candidate, bitten by a dog, must be pretty worthless... I did in the end win a majority in Winchester itself, but that was not enough to overcome the combined votes of villages like Bentworth. I could take some comfort that the team led so ably by my agent, Tessa Fothergill, won 41 per cent of the vote cast and had made Winchester constituency winnable.

45 Improving Winchester?

It was just before that election that the Winchester City Council came to have "No Overall Control". It was hung. The five Labour councillors held the balance between the dwindling Tories and the rising Alliance. George Fothergill and I held a meeting with the Tory leader, Georgie Busher from Bishop's Waltham, and John Cloyne, the Labour leader. We came to an agreement that Georgie would lead the council and chair the senior committee for Policy and Resources, George would be in charge of Amenities, and John would have charge of the Housing Committee. Otherwise, Pat Edwards, an interesting Tory, headed the Planning Committee, and Brian Collins of the Alliance led the Health and Works. I was to be the Deputy Chairman of Housing.

I thoroughly enjoyed my time in harness with John. The previous year I had been invited to chair the Winchester Committee for the International Year of the Homeless. John also served on the committee; through him and others I learnt much about housing in Great Britain. We did, in fact, raise a significant sum of money and work out a strategy for dealing with homelessness in Winchester. There were many people sleeping rough, mostly in the covered car parks. I went with a very able young woman, Mandy Griffiths, around those car parks between midnight and 1.00am counting the dormant bodies. For the international aspect of the year much of the money went to a basic housing project near Delhi. It was just as well that I enjoyed and thought worthwhile what I was doing, because in that same year of 1987 the Alliance split apart. David Owen, the SDP leader who had ousted Roy Jenkins to take that position, could not tolerate working with David Steel, the Liberal leader. All of that became apparent at the Annual SDP September Conference held in Portsmouth. I remember returning home from it with a raging migraine, a condition that I had not experienced since childhood. It was very depressing.

I almost gave up politics. Did I really want to go slogging on through, to what? I even put in for the headmastership of Fettes in Edinburgh, Tony Blair's old school. I was asked up for an interview at the end of November and remember being delighted, as the train went north through East Lothian, to see skeins of pink-footed geese flying parallel to the train. I was in fact excited. Being in the centre of Edinburgh, Fettes, I thought, might have difficulties in expanding if the school wanted to. And so I contacted the Planning Department and became very up to date with what the opportunities and problems were. When the interview came, I was on something of a high and was not surprised to be asked back to be interviewed on the short list. Back home, I had second thoughts. Felicity was not keen and one of the Fettes governors, who lived in London and had been unable to be present at the Edinburgh interview, let us down. We had agreed with him that he and his wife would come down to Winchester to see us in our domestic setting. Felicity loved entertaining and would have been a good headmaster's wife. But the school governor could not come; we were to go to London to lunch at his house. And that was a cold affair. I withdrew, which put Fettes in something of a quandary, as there were only two of us on the final short list.

But there was important work to do in Winchester, especially as my time in the Ecology Party had emphasised "Think Global and Act Local". In the Housing Committee, the officers supporting John Cloyne and myself, Noel Mullins and Andrew Clark, could not have been more helpful. We built such council housing as meagre resources and government restrictions allowed, but we also built a lot in partnership with housing associations. My old Oriel friend, Ken Bartlett, was an inspiration in the background. He had acquired enormous experience with housing associations, having been an innovator in that field when Rachman was doing his worst in the sixties. In 1987 Ken was the Chief Finance Officer in the Housing Corporation. John and I, with Noel and Andrew, worked together for two and a half years, and somehow ensured that during that period more low-cost houses were built in Winchester District than in the whole of London. Or so we were told. I was happy too that Mary Sabben-Clare, the wife of James, the new headmaster of the College, was pleased to be on the committee, chaired by Jeremy Ouvry, which dealt with housing associations. Through them we were able to build much-needed affordable houses in the villages. John and I used to go round the rural parishes to find out what they wanted. Such opposition as there was came mainly from owners of second homes who wanted to avoid disturbance to their newly acquired rural idyll.

The local elections of 1990 saw a change in my councillor's activities. I became the chairman of a new major committee that I had championed – the Engineering Committee, looking after roads, sewers, and similar matters. But first the election itself was interesting. I fought it over Mrs. Thatcher's Poll Tax, admittedly a central government initiative, but one with a grave local effect. It seemed quite extraordinary to me that some well-off people could not see how unfair it was. On one of the farms in my ward there was a family in a tied house working the land. They did not earn much; they had not enjoyed an even passable education. Their local tax was due to rise from £200 per year to £1,900. I remember visiting a member of the House of Lords who had two houses, one in London, and one in my ward. "It's only fair," he said in a most reasonable tone, "that everybody should pay the same." It never occurred to him, and I could not persuade him, that somebody who might easily have been a multi-millionaire should pay more than someone who was close to the breadline. I am pleased to say that in that local election which I fought in "my" ward there was a turn-out of 76 per cent. I secured 68 per cent of that, although the ward had once been a Conservative stronghold. The noble lord was not totally representative of people who normally voted Conservative.

My new role was important to me. The aim was to reduce traffic coming into Winchester and thereby the pollution. The officer in charge of roads and engineering works, David Marklew, and I were in complete accord. So too was the Winchester Preservation Trust. And so we introduced Park and Ride following the example of Oxford and, as a complement to that, residents' parking. There was stiff opposition, but by dint of numerous small local meetings we persuaded enough people for the first stages. Unfortunately a further stage to convert a hidden part of the now grassed-over bypass into a Park and Ride was held up by a romantic green activist who insisted that the scheme meant the destruction of a "wildflower meadow" and the creation of an eyesore seen from St. Catherine's Hill. There was absolutely no possibility of an impending eyesore seen from anywhere on St. Catherine's Hill.

It was not until years after I had ceased sitting on the council that the scheme was enacted; but an important part of the concept, the conversion into housing of car parks in the centre of the city, never came to pass, despite that idea being a plank in the Liberal Democrat overall plan and despite the fact that by that time they controlled the council. Of all the actions that I should not have taken in my life I count this to be the worst: if I had stayed on the council once the Lib Dems had taken it over, I would have been in a position (as the likely leader of the council) to push the whole plan through. That, however, would have taken another seven years, and I was running out of steam. I have often wondered whether people who go into politics see it as an interesting game or hobby. That was certainly the view of one old Liberal councillor; rather an expensive hobby, he thought.

While I was a councillor I was also involved in an important but unpopular conversion of a central car park into a shopping mall with an underground car park. I was on a panel to adjudicate schemes for the project. The scheme that I supported was eventually the scheme chosen. Not many people admired it. It was not helped by coming into fruition just at the time of the economic downturn in the early nineties, and so it was difficult to fill all the shop units.

Nevertheless, the profit that the council received was put to good use. In the Byzantine accounting policies forced on local governments it was possible on the strength of it to pull in permission from Whitehall to build more houses through housing associations. It was also used to bring main drainage to the parishes in the south of the district. One of my last duties was in the southern village of Hambledon, where the game of cricket was invented. The autumn months of 1993 were extraordinarily wet. The hills above Hambledon (topped by the cricket field) began to ooze water. At first it was a trickle, then it became a flood. Water poured down the main street and forced an entry into the cellars of every house. Many of these cellars had been converted into rooms, usually offices with expensive high-tech machines, which were all ruined. Then the water threatened the ground floors. The Winchester Engineering Department and the Fire Department rushed to the rescue, channelling the river into huge pipes to empty the water into a real stream at the bottom of the valley. The inhabitants needed reassurance and so I chaired a crowded meeting to explain what was being done and what would be done. A person sitting in the front row was Bill Organ, who had recently been offered the post of Bursar at Winchester College.

46 A Brush with the Law

Just before I came off the council I was arrested. I had been plotting the victory of my successor as councillor in the ward of Sparsholt and we had shared a half bottle of wine to encourage us to think. I was driving the four miles back home when I decided I needed petrol. Having filled up and paid, I was about to ease away when a dirty white Transit van drew up beside me leaving only the smallest space between it and the podium on which the petrol pump stood. I thought I could squeeze through; and indeed I did – the only problem being that the car mounted the podium. I was pulling away from the filling station when I heard shouts behind me. Back I went to see what was up. Three scruffy young men came towards me.

"You've scratched my car," said the tallest, showing me a long rusty scrape.

"No, I haven't. That scrape is very old, I never hit your car."

"Yes, you did, mate!" At that point he pulled a knife on me, and as I tried to back off to run to the people behind the cash desk, another young man landed a punch on my left eye. I made my escape, the young men came into the shop, but by that time I was in a room behind the desk. They made a lot of noise but then, realising that the police were being summoned, moved back into the van and drove away while we wrote down the van's number. The police arrived, a very large policeman and an even larger policewoman. They began to take details, but then asked: "Have you been drinking, Sir?"

"Yes, two small glasses." They breathalysed me.

"You're under arrest. Get into our car. We're taking you to Eastleigh to check the reading."

Because Winchester's police station was only one mile away and Eastleigh's seven, I remonstrated in my best posh accent: "Look, I've been assaulted. I'm not the one to arrest!"

"Can't help it. You're over the limit. But we'll go to Winchester."

Once at the police station, they put me in a cell. Some ten minutes later they breathalysed me again. The big machine showed that I was some way under the limit. "Right, you can go." So saying, they disappeared. A small, dark-haired rather meek policewoman took their place to give me a lift back to my car.

"Do you like working in the police force?" I asked her in the car.

"No, not very much. They don't see things straight."

"You can say that again!"

We drove back to my car at the filling station. The station's attendants were very sympathetic: "At least the police have the van's number!"

But they never traced the van. Somebody took a photo of my black eye, and I made a statement that the blow had put "floaters" into my eye. The *Hampshire Chronicle* reported that an elderly man had been assaulted at the Weeke filling station. I thought of making an official complaint, but decided that I had other things to do.

DIFFERENT OCCUPATIONS, 1994–2001

47 A Novel in the Dark

I now started on my sabbatical. I had thought to spend it in Ithaca and write a novel that I had in my head, with inspiration derived from the shade of the one-time king of Ithaca, Odysseus. But Roger was ill and needed to spend the winter in England. Macina was obviously the best place to be; it would be cheaper and I would not have to take time to find my feet. The novel was clearly ready to be written. It would contain a rough mixture of my experiences, my reading and environmental views. Indeed I completed it in ten weeks, and that included a final revision.

I enjoyed the process, no doubt a process that real novelists go through as a routine. Since Macina's only artificial light worked, spasmodically, on a gas cylinder, I wrote during the hours of daylight. I rose from my bed and ate my breakfast before dawn. I worked in two-hour spells on my old-fashioned Hermes typewriter in front of the window looking towards the castle on the opposite hill. At the beginning of each spell I revised what I had written in the previous spell: about two sides of A4. Then I would produce another two sides. Since I was totally on my own, at ten o'clock I would go down to the village by car for a "sanity break" and buy something from Paolo and Marinella's. That involved a chat. Returning before eleven o'clock I sat down for another two hours before breaking off for lunch. In the afternoon I sometimes took my Formica table to work on the hillside in the sun. The sheep would come and inspect me. The first time this happened, my head was down, hard at work. I looked up. I was surrounded by sheep. The nearest ones were scarcely three feet away. Their approach had been totally silent. Nor as they looked at me with faintly amused expressions did they shuffle their feet or start bleating. I felt honoured.

My afternoon sessions ended promptly at four. Then I collected wood for the fire before darkness fell, at about four-thirty in late November. Once the fire was lit, I sat down under the gas lamp with a bottle of whisky or flagon of wine beside me to read books. The heat of the fire went mostly up the huge chimney. Near the end of the year the cold really set in. Then I pulled a sleeping bag round my body to read actually inside the hearth with the fire blazing away and losing most of its heat up the chimney. I read lots of books; fat books, thin books, paperbacks and hardbacks; novels, historical books, political books and environmental books. (I rather turned up my nose at detective fiction.) I cannot remember all the books I read, but they did include *Middlemarch, A Suitable Boy, The Bridge over the River Drina, Pagans and Christians in the Mediterranean* by Robin Lane Fox, and Misha Glenny on Yugoslavia and its disintegration. After that intellectual stimulation and several glasses, I swayed into the kitchen next door, cooked my supper by candlelight and ate it, drinking more local wine while conversing with the characters in my novel. They were surprisingly chatty and gave me several lines to follow up the next day. By nine o'clock I was ready to go to bed.

Actually, I was not totally alone. I usually took a day off a week, visiting Florence, Rome, Pienza, and Perugia. I was also visited from time to time by Augusto, better known as Augu. Augu used the farm below for his flock of sheep, the very ones that visited me. He looked after the land for a group of devotees of Hari Krishna who now owned it. We had known each other for some time. He visited me in the evening after he had visited his sheep. He would bring me wine that he had made, ricotta from his sheep, and a small paraffin heater. That was when it became very cold, and he said that he did not want me to suffer frostbite. Augu was a shy, limited, middle-aged man who had been sent as a scholarship boy to a Jesuit boarding school near Siena. I don't know what happened there, but it was not good. He was certainly intelligent, but very limited in his emotions. Recent revelations about Roman Catholic boarding schools are not reassuring.

But Augu was kind. We celebrated my fifty-sixth birthday together in a cavernous restaurant in Viterbo. Apparently his patron, a wealthy art historian at Rome University, had once taken him there. He also asked me to help with the olive harvest at the beginning of December. It was a sunny day; he and his friend Attico, talking in an incomprehensible dialect, picked the olives by hacking and pruning the trees first and taking the fruit off the branches when they lay on the ground. I enjoyed the experience and the fantasy that I was in the company of Augustus, the Emperor of Rome, and Atticus, the famous epistolary correspondent of Cicero.

My other social experience was provided by Nigel and Cathy Anderson who had decided to visit me for Christmas. They were extremely brave. They arrived on Christmas Eve when it was snowing lightly and the temperature was below freezing. We kept warm by lighting the gas oven in the kitchen and sitting in front of it. But Christmas day was beautifully sunny. We went to Assisi where the snow had already thawed in the town, but it had covered the great mound of Monte Subasio in a spotless and dazzling white. Despite our lack of religious belief, we spent time communing with eternity in the crypt of St. Francis under the double-tiered basilica that was built to house his earthly remains. On Boxing Day we visited the Etruscan necropolises of Cerveteri and Tarquinia close to the sea. By then, at sea level, it was hot enough for us to be happily refreshed under the domes of Etruscan tombs. Nigel was especially happy; he is a classical architect with Robert Adam and a descendent of the intrepid, first Etruscologist, George Dennis.

The visit to Assisi was well timed. I had been inspired by a medieval fresco that was being uncovered in the private chapel of the grand "big" house in San Michele. When I visited it earlier in my stay, enough had been revealed to show that St. Francis was the main figure, but that there would be another figure to his right still covered by whitewash. I thought about this and decided that it would suit my novel to put in a similar scene, with St. Clare (aka Santa Chiara) standing out in the open with St. Francis, instead of being confined in a nunnery. Clearly my fifteenth-century squire of the village had heretical views; perhaps it was for that reason that the fresco had been covered up in the Counter Reformation of the seventeenth century…

Soon after the departure of Nigel and Cathy on the day after Boxing Day I left Italy to arrive back in Winchester in time for the New Year and a new school term. The novel? A friend, a published novelist in her own right, looked at what I had written and found its narrator to be infuriatingly smug. He was put in a drawer to await his fate, and he is still there. Another novelist did say that a first effort should never be shown to a novelist.

48 Second Master at Winchester College: 1994–2001

I was now somewhat under-employed. I did play a small part in the selection and consequent electioneering of Mark Oaten, my successor but one, as parliamentary candidate in Winchester for the Liberal Democrats. Mark was a good candidate; he listened well, he worked extremely hard to get to know and support his would-be constituents. He also had a good knowledge of politics and Westminster, partly from his work as a lobbyist. It was only that profession that made me wonder whether his convictions were serious enough about the path that the UK was taking.

The count for his election in 1997 was electric. After several recounts, making Winchester the last constituency to declare, in the evening of the day after the election he managed to depose the sitting Tory, Gerry Malone, by two votes. Much depended on spoilt ballot papers. There was one in particular that I remember: a paper with a huge diagonal cross spreading across the four corners with its centre happening to fall in the Conservative box. Was it a spoilt ballot paper, with the voter wishing to register a dislike of all the candidates? Or was it a vote for the Conservatives? Whatever the case, the Conservatives disputed the result. Which was very unwise. Recently in Winchester they had disputed close local election results, but in the reruns they had been trounced. In November, therefore, a Lib Dem majority of two became a majority of some 22,000. Bad losers are not appreciated, it seems.

Otherwise, I had a full teaching timetable and was in charge of all divs and div dons in the sixth form. That had its problems. One div don, who was also in charge of a house, needed a lot of help, often in the small hours of the morning. But he refused to see that he was close to a nervous breakdown. The management found it a difficult situation. I was also a listening ear for the matrons who worked in the boarding houses. Theirs was often a rewarding job, but hard too. They could find themselves marooned, as it were, in a male society.

Within two years, without any warning, I was invited by the Warden, Jeremy Morse, to become the Second Master. This was a post that originally meant being in charge of the fourteenth-century scholars' house, College. But now as a result of the school becoming bigger and of an increased need for administration, the post stood free of housemasterly duties. I took time to decide. The post was likely to be onerous. James Sabben-Clare was due to retire after three more years; I would go next, the following year. In the meantime I would be seeing in a new headmaster. I took myself off to a well-man clinic. The results were good. And so I accepted.

James and I had always been friendly but never close. However, my time in Winchester City politics had given me a certain perspective which possibly commended me to him and to Bill Organ, the Bursar. The Bursar reported directly to the Warden and not to the headmaster. The two did not find the situation easy; I might have been seen as a go-between.

James had been at Winchester almost all his life, apart from his time at a Yorkshire preparatory school, New College, a year at All Souls, and a brief spell at Marlborough. He had a very good brain. At the age of thirteen he was the top scholar at Winchester. He also won the top classics scholarship to New College, followed by a double first. His ambition was to be headmaster of Winchester. And he progressed resolutely towards it through his time as Head of Classics and Second Master in

College. He had a powerful champion in Lord Aldington who was the Warden before Jeremy Morse. Aldington remembered his old school days when the Second Master, Monty Rendell, had become a much-admired headmaster. In 1985 James had the choice of becoming the head of either Rugby or Winchester. He chose Winchester. It was perhaps not the better choice. He knew Winchester very well and was himself well known, but he lacked experience of other places and sometimes gave the impression of lacking confidence with people. His competitor for Winchester would have been in place for only seven years. If he had gone to Rugby, he could easily have come back to Winchester and made a fresh start. James was a kind, good man, a fair man, a determined man. He was well organised, had a good memory and was much liked by his pupils. But he would have profited from more experience elsewhere.

Jeremy Morse, when he interviewed me, asked me what my priority would be as Second Master. I answered that I would want to make good contact with the members of the staff. If they felt that they were listened to, they would teach and look after their pupils all the better. And so that was my aim. As a part of that I also had to reacquaint myself with the school. For twelve years my time there had been spent almost exclusively in the classroom. I also needed to become more familiar with computers and the internet. I had been so busy combining teaching with politics that I had been left behind by all the advances in technology since 1980.

A pleasant house, that had once been a shop, went with the post. It was neither too big nor too small, nor was it too grand. If people wanted to see me, it was a good place for them to come to. For the most part I went to see them on their own ground. That could be housemasters in their houses, the school caterer in his or her office, the boatman, who looked after rowing, in his boathouse, or teachers in their houses. That meant wandering around, which would include soccer and cricket fields for matches, the swimming pool and gymnasia, the art school and the theatre, and other places too. One of those places was the Treasury.

Over the years the College had acquired and been given artefacts of considerable interest and value. Its collection of Chinese porcelain, Ancient Greek pottery, stained glass, and replicas of famous statues made it the best collection south of the Thames. These objects were housed and displayed for the public in what had been the College's old beer cellar, a magnificent, semi-underground, medieval vaulted space, not unlike a cathedral chapter house. Unfortunately, as a result of the Children's Act of 1989, it had become more and more difficult to give access to the public. The space was also too constricted. The keeper of the Treasury, John Falconer, was exercised by this problem. My background in art and planning made me interested in it too. So together we devised a scheme to change the Warden's Stables, which housed little except a few bicycles, into a new Treasury. It would be more spacious than its predecessor and easier for the public to visit. The plan took a long time before it was put into action. But after my retirement John worked tirelessly to make it happen, liaising with experts and, perhaps most important, the Bursary. It became a key aspect of a fundraising campaign. It caught the imagination of Old Wykehamists and was seen as a "loss leader" into more prosaic, though no less important, projects such as raising money for bursaries. The idea was mooted in 2000 and completed in 2016. The outcome is magnificent.

My office was an important place for me. With the Bursary I found myself having to devise official policies for health and safety, the Children's Act, and the induction and training of new teachers, particularly those who had not followed an official teacher training course. What took a lot of time and such diplomacy as I could muster was the management of the relationship of the boarding houses and housemasters with the Bursary. The Bursar (rightly, up to a point) was trying to streamline their activities. The housemasters (rightly, up to a point) were trying to hold on to practices which they thought helped the family atmosphere of their houses. Discipline was another area. Because the school is close to the town, boys could sneak out, go to the pubs, or find someone who would sell them a joint. "Duty" dons were supposed every now and again to make town visits in the evening to discourage wayward behaviour. This was a very unpopular duty, and so I would quite frequently go out with them. At meetings of the Common Room which happened every Wednesday morning at break, it was often my lot to say something about DISCIPLINE! I gave myself the soubriquet of the "Dreary Dragon". It was after James had retired and the arrival of the new headmaster that this became difficult.

49 Finding a New Headmaster, 1999

(Population – 6 billion; CO2 ppm – 367; Centigrade – + 1.0)

The Governing Body had not found it easy to appoint a new headmaster. Two trawls had been necessary. The situation was not helped by the illness in its early stages of the Warden, Lord Younger, who had succeeded Jeremy Morse, but had still kept the chairmanship of the Royal Bank of Scotland. I had the impression of some disarray. On the second trawl they made a bold appointment, of Dr. Nicholas Tate, the Chief Executive of the Qualifications and Curriculum

Authority. This body reported to the Secretary of State for Education on matters to do with public examinations. Dr. Tate had not, in fact, taught in a classroom for at least thirty years, far less in an independent boarding school. But he was an able man, and as his number two, I liked him.

But there were difficulties. There was a new boy, rather older than most new boys, who had arrived recently. He was very well known to Nick from before he came, but he caused a lot of trouble committing almost every offence possible at a school, despite excellent pastoral handling by his housemaster and the chaplain. Eventually, the crisis came; the boy had involved several others in a big drugs affair. The timing was awkward, four weeks before the school broke up for the summer holidays, four weeks indeed before I was due to retire. It was the weekend when the Warden and Fellows were in residence for official meetings. On the Friday morning before Chapel I met Nick as we did every weekday. I said to him that we should think of the boy going to another school. That would help him to wipe the slate clean and start again, an action that can work with difficult pupils. I have never in my life seen someone's face turn so black. "If he goes, I go." And the meeting came to an abrupt end.

We both went to chapel. I thought very hard on my knees: it was well known that finding a new headmaster had been difficult for the College. If that headmaster departed within a year…? I also had to think of myself and my imminent retirement. Could I sensibly stay on as an interim headmaster? I was tired, my own daughter was separating from her husband, and my sister in Herefordshire was in a coma. Might the problem possibly resolve itself? Miracles can happen, can they? I decided that the boy should be given one more chance; the summer holidays were coming, and Nick and the boy's mother would have time to think. At least Nick knew now, if he had not known already, how desperate the situation was. I told Nick of my decision and gave him my backing when we met in the evening with the Warden and Fellows.

In the short term there was no miracle. Within two years Nick had left and the boy was found guilty of arson and bound over. Perhaps in the end he'll be a recognised genius and a force for good.

CHAOS and THE AGE OF AQUARIUS, 2001–2016

50 The Year AD 2001

I retired in the first year of the third millennium. Turns of centuries have often been seen as game changers, and turns of millennia even more so. The year AD 1000 was awaited with the fear that the Last Trump would sound. This new millennium of ours was heralded by some astrologers as the beginning of the Age of Aquarius, an age of invention and generosity but also of chaos. It was taking over from the Age of Pisces that had started at about the same time as the life of Jesus. The next age will be the Age of Capricorn from AD 4000 onwards – not that humans will necessarily be there to experience it. Astrologers are in fact divided about the starting date of the Age of Aquarius, with some taking it back as far as 1780, a year that more or less corresponds to the USA's Declaration of Independence or the commencement of the Industrial Revolution.

Whatever the case, the first year of the new century and new millennium witnessed a terrible and unprecedented act. The mainland of the USA and two of its major cities were attacked. Passenger jets were flown straight into the walls of the Pentagon and the Twin Towers of the World Trade Center in New York. The sight of those planes hurtling into the Twin Towers could actually be witnessed round the world. I was taking a bath at the time when Carlina telephoned from London: "Dad, have you seen the plane crashing into the WTC?" I bundled myself into my dressing gown and switched on the television. Carlina was still on the phone: "Look! Here's another one going into the other tower! Isn't it just awful!" Yes, it was there on the screen, the plane bashing straight into the skyscraper. Though terrorist attacks had recently been made on US embassies abroad, nothing like this had happened in the USA itself since the day before my third birthday seventy years earlier when I heard my father cry out at the news on the wireless about Pearl Harbour. And Pearl Harbour was on the coast of an island thousands of miles away from Washington. Nor had such an act been so publicly witnessed while it was taking place.

The newly elected President of the USA reacted. Troops were sent to Afghanistan, the training ground for the terrorists, and over the centuries the graveyard of incoming armies. Not content with that, eighteen months later his administration implicated Iraq in what they seem to have interpreted as a general Middle Eastern conspiracy. Saddam Hussein was developing (it was thought) nuclear weapons. The evidence was flimsy, but nevertheless the UK's prime minister was persuaded, war was declared despite the huge public marches in London. And so, for many nights thereafter television screens across the world were lit up by the flashes of thunderous explosions from cruise missiles raining down on Baghdad. There was a widespread suspicion that the American government wanted control of the Iraqi oil fields. Twenty years on, the war in Afghanistan is coming to an ignominious end, there are still prisoners held in concentration camps on the coast of Cuba, and Muslim countries from Pakistan, through Syria (not forgetting Israel) to Tunisia are wracked by uncertainty, if not by all-out violence.

51 A New Partner and Life in an Italian Village

At the very time when Baghdad was being bombarded, Jane and I moved into a new home. To live together. Soon to be married. Jane is my partner in life, and I love her dearly. She's vivacious, pretty, funny and great company – and a wonderful cook.

We had waited a long time to get together. Felicity and I had parted some years earlier, but in such a way that we kept in contact, were friendly, and thought about our two daughters together. That was made easier because we all lived in Winchester, and still do. Felicity had kept the big house which she and I had bought but had never possessed enough money properly to renovate. I had moved into a little bow-shaped top-storey flat high above the centre of the town from where (when I was responsible for the traffic in the city) I could see whether vehicles on the road were moving smoothly or whether they were all jammed up, now that there were so many cars coming into the city off the M3. Eventually Felicity and her partner, Rob, sold the big house for a good price and Jane and I found a cosy terraced house, conveniently close to the dentists, the doctors, the well-stocked corner shop, and the railway station. It also possessed a gem of a small, slightly irregular, walled garden, which only became a gem when Jane drew out and amplified all its possibilities, planting a fig tree here, an elderflower there, a winter-flowering cherry, and a once-tiny, rabbit-nibbled magnolia grandiflora. Beneath them the borders were full of colour from a multitude of flowers and at the end of the garden an archway was festooned with climbing roses and clematis to hide the dustbins at the back. In the summer the sunny patio close to the house, where we ate our lunches, was filled with the scent of jasmine.

Jane's father had served in the navy and he and her mother had moved round the world, living in Malta and Mauritius when Jane was a teenager. After marrying Robbie, who also for a short time was in the navy, she had spent some years living on the coasts of Scotland and Wales, near Faslane for the navy, and gaining much renown as a master chef in Wales. And so she had made only brief holiday forays into Western Europe. Because Felicity was now the sole owner of Macina and Jane had a desire to have a more permanent place in another European country, we decided to see what France had to offer. Jane speaks good French, learnt mostly from boyfriends in Mauritius, and I knew the basics and was more than happy to improve on that. I had discovered from earlier visits to France that I was particularly welcomed when I revealed that I was a Scot and not English, which I rather enjoyed. Living in another country and being able to speak the language does add a wider dimension to life.

And so, once our small terraced house in Winchester had been made habitable, we accepted an offer from Shirley, Roger Montgomery's sister, to house-sit in the eccentric château of Fosseuse which her husband, Jean Loup, had inherited from an uncle. The uncle had bought the estate for its shooting and intended to knock the château down. But the war intervened, the château survived, and Jean Loup as a boy cycled all the way north from the centre of Nazi-occupied Paris to enjoy its tranquillity. Thus he fell in love with it.

It is a fascinating sixteenth-century, Henri Quatre, tall, oblong château. When we were there, we saw pigeons flying into the fifth floor at the top of the house through broken window panes. The fourth floor too was strewn with rubble, though it was gradually being renovated. The third floor had three grand bedrooms, newly restored, for paying guests. The family lived on the second floor, in rooms made habitable by the insertion of prefabricated units, and the ground floor consisted of a kitchen and a huge living space with massive oak beams, dark and heavy antique French furniture, and at one end an imposing baronial fireplace. Long ago it had been the chateau's kitchen.

The spacious grounds were well suited to shooting. Thick woods around the perimeter provided homes for pheasants, deer and boar, and wild duck visited the large carp pond in the middle of which was an untidy, wooded island where they nested. There was also a largely disused L-shaped farmstead that housed broken-down wooden wagons and rusty harrows. Somewhere in the woods there was an old underground ice house for the preservation of game. To enjoy all this we had asked friends to stay the fortnight with us. Alas, the day before we set off Shirley rang up. She had broken a leg. She and Jean Loup would not be going down to Toulon where they kept an old boat. Why don't we come and stay anyway? We decided not to. Our friends were able to do something else and Peter Partner let us borrow his house in Giove, fifty miles north of Rome. Thus started for me a second sojourn in Italy, and for Jane her first.

Jane fell in love with that part of Italy – my part of Italy. She had never been to the middle reaches of the Tiber Valley nor to the hilltop towns of Umbria, nor to the burial chambers of the Etruscans in Lazio, let alone the volcanic mountains and lakes. And so, we decided to have a house not in France, but there in Lazio. It helped our decision that small Italian houses were cheaper than their counterparts in France. And so, after a second stay in the Partners' Giove home, and much helped by Augu and by my old pupil and cultural guru, Nigel McGilchrist, who lived near Orvieto, we found a house for 40,000 euros which would have cost £400,000 in Winchester. It was on the edge of the hilltop village of Sermugnano, looking over a cliff down to Castiglione in Teverina and the long, middle stretch of the Tiber Valley. Once it was bought we were so thrilled that we decided to spend New Year's Eve there. For this house was not as primitive as Macina. It had mains gas, electricity, a modern openable stove that heated the whole house, and had been beautifully renovated by the vendor, Marco Centoscudi. His reason for leaving? His Lithuanian wife was hankering after the bright lights of a city. She found Sermugnano too isolated and dull.

Northern Europe was blanketed with snow as we motored south. We were greeted by bright sunlight in Italy, and freezing cold. The house however was snug and warm. Marco had made sure that our fire was blazing away. What's more we were invited to celebrate New Year's Eve with the Centoscudi family, some of whom we had already met when we were buying the house. The party was in Marco's parents' flat at the top of the main palazzo in the piazza which was owned by the local council. The parents, Lillo and Gabriela, were delightful and full of fun. Their children and their partners were all there: Loris and Donatella, Monia and Fabrizio, Marco and Alina. Then their grandchildren, Giuseppe and Francesca, Fabio and Bianca, and Dennis (Alina's son) – fifteen in all, filling Gabriela's sitting/dining/kitchen, a decent-sized little room, but far from large. The meal, however, was very large: antipasti of local salames, mortadella and salsicci, followed by tagliatelle ai funghi, followed by dorada, followed by wild boar stew (Gabriela's speciality) followed by pecorino cheese, all washed down with litres of Donatella's father's red wine. Italians don't on the whole drink much, but Lillo did, and I, not being Italian, drank a lot. There was a great deal of noise. We sang national anthems amidst general agreement that the Marseillaise was the best. I talked rather too much in my not-very-good Italian. The Centoscudis chattered away shouting across the table. I understood very little, Jane understood nothing. But the mood was one of laughter, so who cared? The Centoscudis loved having us, and we loved being their guests. At midnight we went outside to watch the fireworks in the Tiber Valley.

We stood just outside the piazza, where there was a view. It was a glitteringly black, freezing night, with the Milky Way littering the sky above us. Down in the valley the lights of all the little towns sparkled so clearly and out of them soared and crackled the New Year rockets, one after the other. It was a bitterly cold, memorable New Year's Eve.

We lived in Sermugnano for the next twelve years, each year for two spells of some four weeks. We came to know many people. The Centoscudis obviously. We were on calling terms with Lillo and Gabriela. We would drop in on them. They came and sat on our capacious upper terrace outside our bedroom at the top of the house overlooking the small green valley immediately below, where wild boar would forage of an evening beneath two cherry trees. Lillo would regale us with stories of hunting the boar or how in the Second World War British planes flew over the area to bomb the railway bridge that crossed the Tiber in the narrow gorge below the nearby village of Baschi, and how they never succeeded, but got shot down by the Nazis; then how the villagers took them in and hid them in their caves, except they always drank too much wine and sang raucous songs which gave them and their saviours away, so that they were all shot.

All this he said with some obvious exaggeration and a twinkle in his eye while we downed the wine he had brought with him. Gabriela and I played up to this, and so did Jane having rapidly to learn colloquial Italian. The two of them were in fact illiterate. Their children were not. Marco was well travelled, superb in his craft. He and Alina went off to live in Viterbo, where the bright lights lured her away from him. Loris worked on the trunk roads; he and Donatella had a house beside her father's vineyards. Monia lived in Rome where Fabrizio was one of ENEL's top electrical engineers.

There was also the extended Centoscudi family, Lillo's brothers: Silvano who could turn his hand to anything constructional, like laying the paving outside the bottom of our house. There was Giuliano who had worked with the railways and retired in his fifties. His wife, Franca, was a prolific reader of novels and came to be the mainstay of our house. While we were away she watered the geraniums and jasmine that Jane had planted in pots on the upper terrace, and she also opened and closed the windows to make sure that the house kept dry. We came to know Lidia and Navino who owned the village shop in the piazza and kept it going as a service to the village. Other people living elsewhere were often to be seen: the retired Secretary to the National Treasury, Augusto, who knew Lillo and Gabriela, and Andrea who drove swish buses for tourists and his wealthy American girlfriend, Joanna. Georg, a law professor from Frankfurt, with his wife Birgit, had long owned a house on the other side of the road from us and similarly it was the last house in the village before one looked over the cliff. We enjoyed the company of all these people and they seemed to enjoy ours; we once gave a sit-down supper for twenty-six on Silvano's patio, taking – as it were – our turn to make the village a festive place.

For, in fact, it was rather a sad village. Twenty years earlier it had a population of 300. Now only fifty remained permanently, though in the summer holidays the figure doubled when people came back to the village of their childhood. It had the air of a town, this village. A large church with a converted convent behind it stood at one end of the oval piazza. At the other end a winding street led up to a small castle and another road led down to our house. The castle was divided into flats and had its own church, and on the lower road there was a beautiful small fourteenth-century Romanesque chapel. At some time in the sixties property owners must have thought the place had potential and so built two tall palazzi beside the lower road. The piazza itself enclosed by tall curving buildings would not have been out of place in Rome. There was a sort of sad pride in the village; Marcello, the village builder, concentrated his skills on restoring houses that then lay empty, although a slow infiltration of Romanians offered some hope of an increased population. They were not entirely welcome, they tended to untidiness; but the natives of Sermugnano were typical enough of Italians south of the industrial cities to put on a smiling face of acceptance.

We lived a leisurely, not uncreative life in Sermugnano. We did our shopping mainly in Orvieto, paid our taxes in Castiglione where we banked, and went frequently to Lidia's shop for odds and ends. We explored a lot, visiting places that I knew, but many that I did not, like the famous gardens at Nimfa and La Foce, Iris Origo's gardens in the Val d'Orcia where her daughter, Benedetta, still lived. Journeys from and to Winchester gave us the chance to visit French cathedrals and chateaus, spend time at the Villa Belvedere, the lovely hotel in Argegno on the shores of Lake Como, and off the coast of Liguria watch from a boat plying its scheduled journey past the ancient piratical villages of the Cinque Terre an unending line of Japanese tourists trudging conscientiously, visiting every village on the way. Tired of motoring such distances, latterly we took the ferry from Barcelona in Spain to Rome's port at Civitavecchia, which gave us a taste of that famous Catalan city to compare with those cities we knew better. But much of the time we were near to home. In the summer we often went swimming on the north shore of Lake Bolsena, near the little town of Bolsena itself, which now, compared to forty years earlier, looked so much more like a Rapallo or a Santa Margherita in their heyday.

But we enjoyed our house: the sunshine on our upper terrace, the view of Castiglione rising like an island out of the autumn mists in the Tiber Valley, the song of nightingales on April evenings. We spent a lot of time reading. I was extremely aware of the almost imperceptible but steady advance of climate change and environmental degradation, feeling sad and almost guilty that I had achieved little before I gave up my political work. Many of the books that I read were on that theme. We also worked on the house, turning the wine-cantina on the lowest floor of the house into a cool bedroom for guests – or for us when the bedroom at the top of the house became too hot. We put in shutters and mosquito nets over the windows, cleared out the cave to give order to our clutter and make room for piles of fire wood, planted olive trees beside

Silvano's patio as well as planting and training a luxuriously abundant Felicita e Perpetua rose to climb up the high wall of the house beside the cave.

But for all that Sermugnano was not as important to us as Winchester.

52 Ancient Winchester

At the turn of the millennia the special school at Lankhills was demolished to make way for private houses and a refurbished special school. This resulted in more fourth-century graves being uncovered to the north of the area where the Winchester schools had excavated thirty years earlier. As one who had played a big part in the earlier dig, I was interested and in 2004/5 made several practical visits to help the young women and men working professionally for Oxford Archaeology. Archaeological skills and techniques had moved on in the intervening years in ways that I barely understood, but clearly there was no substitute for the careful scraping of the soil with a builder's trowel. However, of particular interest and importance, it was now possible by chemical analysis of bone collagen and isotopes in teeth to know more about the origin of the people buried in the cemetery. There was a great deal of variation within the sample taken for analysis. Some were of local origin but a significant number were born far away in North Africa or Eastern Europe. These findings confirmed the increasingly established view of the experts that the people buried in this particular cemetery in Winchester were different from those buried elsewhere in the city and indeed from those buried in cemeteries of the same era excavated elsewhere in Britain. It was already well known that Lankhills was unusually rich in artefacts compared to the other cemetery sites. And now the earlier hypothesis that it contained soldiers from elsewhere was receiving further confirmation. All this was collated in an attractive book published quickly by Oxford Archaeology in 2010.

I had written a chapter for Giles Clarke's book on the earlier dig, which was published in 1979. In it I had tried to extract what I could about the beliefs of the people burying their dead. Of unusual interest was what lay behind the custom of decapitating people before burying them. The seven instances of this rite were all found either close to or actually inside the grave of another, seemingly important, person, of either military or some other high status origin, shown by the inclusion of knives or military belts or piles of coins and other objects. An example was that cenotaph dated to a time soon after AD 400, which I personally had excavated thirty years earlier.

From the evidence we had reckoned that it was some form of human sacrifice. This was not a view that found favour with many people. The evidence for ritual decapitation across the Roman province of Britannia was exhaustively analysed, but the contextual evidence at Lankhills was never found to have been repeated – except in the second excavations at Lankhills. But in Oxford Archaeology's book the contextual evidence was not examined, partly because it was wrongly illustrated in diagram and partly because it was just overlooked. I have found myself trying to understand the thought processes why this should have been the case.

There was, I think, a combination of reasons. The first was that the authors of the report were not the same as the people who supervised the digging; they did not have an intimate knowledge of the site. There is also, perhaps, a parallel in government, where the man in Whitehall does not understand the special circumstances that may exist in Winchester or Wakefield. Experts on the Roman Empire could quote, quite correctly, that human sacrifice was forbidden in the empire. But the more local context seems not to have been taken into account: the people using this seemingly military cemetery were experiencing a time of military and social collapse, much uncertainty about their future, and such psychological stresses that might have been the result. To us amateurs and schoolchildren it did seem a bit bizarre that human sacrifice may have been taking place. And it is possible that the expert archaeologists, coming to the site for the second dig, thought: "It is just like schoolchildren to jump to such a conclusion" – a view which, in my ruminations at the time, I thought I should take into consideration. But the only way to get close to a conclusion was to look at the evidence in its narrowest and widest contexts and to have a thorough appreciation of one's own predetermined thought processes. In the end I decided that the schoolchildren were right. More recently I have come to the view that, in the wider fields of politics and economics, evidence-based conclusions must include a knowledge of one's own predetermined thought processes.

To many people archaeology means "finding things", whether by means of a metal detector or the choosing of 100 objects by the Curator of the British Museum to illustrate the historical period the objects represent. The two objects I would choose from the two excavations at Lankhills would be a gaming set from the early fourth century found in the first excavation, and two related objects from one very late grave in the second excavation. They were a horseman's spur and a cross-bow brooch designed to prevent the horseman's billowing cloak from flying away. On this brooch there was an inscription in Latin "*utere felix*", which means (roughly) "be successful wearing this".

After the Oxford Archaeology monograph was published, Martin Biddle kindly gave me space to express my views on its treatment of decapitations in *The People of Early Winchester (Winchester Studies, Vol 9 i),* a volume that gives all the skeletal details of all the people uncovered in the first excavation and in excavations of Anglo-Saxon cemeteries near Winchester, plus all the instances of decapitation found in each of the excavations at Lankhills.

53 Years of Tension, Climate Change in Numbers

Other events of 2005 made me twitchy. Mark Oaten, Winchester's MP, while challenging for the leadership of the Liberal Democrats exposed himself to sexual blackmail. For the next five years he lost all his verve and energy and the one political party that had signed up to taking climate change seriously was seriously weakened. More immediately important was the coincidence of the G8 conference in Gleneagles and the organised terrorist attacks on London's Underground and public buses. Tony Blair had arranged that the conference should take a serious look at climate change, but before that part of the agenda could be discussed he hurried off to give support to the capital.

A wonderful advantage of the two little houses that I successively owned above the Tiber Valley was that I could read at leisure and contemplate what I read, whether they were novels, or historical, or philosophical, religious even, or books about climate change. As it was climate change that was creeping up inexorably, it was books on that subject that were very much to the fore. I quickly looked again at the books I had read in the early seventies while the M3 was beginning to be pushed through the water meadows around Winchester. There were *Enough is Enough* by John Taylor, our very own Bishop of Winchester, *Small is Beautiful* by E. F. Schumacher, or most seminal of all, *Only One Earth* by René Dubos and Barbara Ward. There were also books ten years later, when I was first involved in politics: *The Brandt Report* and the really prophetic book, years before its time, by Jonathon Porritt, *Seeing Green,* which challenged the emphasis in economics on GDP and growth. After I left politics and had written the novel that is still languishing in a drawer I was influenced by my younger daughter, Alessia, who was studying for a master's degree in Environmental and Development Studies at SOAS in London. She enticed me into an excellent lecture by Philip Stott who regarded climate change as a Golden Age myth, and into reading two books that were on her academic list, Richard D. North's *Life on a Modern Planet* and *Modern Environmentalism* by David Pepper.

Now, however, in 2006, when the situation was looking serious and nobody with any power seemed to be taking it seriously, three extremely important books were published: *The Revenge of Gaia* by James Lovelock, *The Last Generation* by Fred Pearce, and *The Meaning of the 21st Century* by James Martin. Lovelock had already written books on what he called the Gaia Principle meaning that for the last 12,000 years the planet Earth has developed the habit of keeping its ecosystems in balance, but in this book he stressed that the proliferation of human activity was threatening the balance and Gaia would take its "revenge". Pearce's book was on the same theme; even *The Daily Telegraph* backed the opinion of Professor Lord May that "This is a powerful book about the most important event in human history. Read it." In his book, James Martin looked at all the possible threats that the human race and the planet will experience, including first and foremost climate change, then global pandemics and nuclear warfare, and he came to the conclusion that we humans are, as it were, adrift on a fast-flowing river about to enter the rapids in a canyon from which we will emerge chastened and changed, hugely helped by the ever-increasing power of information technology.

By this time I was keeping a tally on the three rising numbers that seemed to indicate the direction that the world was taking. Like many people I had been aware for a long time of the rise in the number of humans inhabiting the planet. The numbers go somewhat like this: in 1800, there were just under 1 billion, a number that had stayed more or less steady for 800 years with a few ups and downs created by Black Death and other plagues. In 1927 there were 2 billion, in 1938 (the year of my birth) there were 2.3 billion, in 1960 (while I was in my third year at university) 3 billion, in 1974 (when the M3 was being planned round Winchester and I was now aware of the escalating number) 4 billion, in 1987 (when I was standing seriously for Parliament) 5 billion, in 1999 (when I was Number Two at Winchester College) 6 billion. By the time I came to write this paragraph 7 billion had been exceeded in 2011, with 8 billion being forecast for 2022. Humans are swarming. The population of Europe is actually coming down right now, but Europe consumes so much of what the Earth produces, both sustainably and unsustainably, that its environmental footprint is about the equivalent of 3 billion. One difficulty about a swarming global population is that many more people will, understandably, want to emulate the rich nations of North America and Europe and indulge in even more unsustainable consumption.

A more difficult figure is the number of particles per million (ppm) there are of CO_2 in the atmosphere. As the thickness of the blanket that CO_2 puts round the Earth affects the temperature of the Earth, any increase in the padding provided by these particles is very important. In 1800 the figure was about 280ppm and had been for a very long time. In 2005 (just before I was reading those three books) it was 379ppm, and now (in 2021) it is 415. The data comes most notably from scientific stations on mountain tops, the best known of which is Mt. Mauna Loa in Hawaii. Humanity over its lifespan of 300,000 years has never existed under such a thick blanket, with the result that the overall temperature of the globe is hotter than humanity has ever experienced.

The figures for the corresponding increase in heat seem very small, but are nevertheless extremely significant. I was not as aware of them in 2006 as I am now, but in 2018 scientists reckoned it was dangerous if the figure reached 1.5 degrees Celsius warmer than in the Industrial Revolution. In 1900 it was 0.3 degrees C warmer, in 1970 0.6 degrees C, in 2000 0.9 degrees C, and in 2021 1.15 degrees C warmer.

Just as there had been an unfortunate conjunction of important matters in 2005, a similar occurrence happened three years later. In 2008 the UK Climate Change Act was passed; the Labour government was taking notice. But the Act was overshadowed by the sub-prime mortgage scandal in US banks that caused the major recession of the next two years. The collapse of the global financial system was averted only by the use of quantitative easing, which in turn greatly magnified the gap in the world between the rich and the poor that had already been growing for some years. It also bedevilled forward thinking, so that when the Labour government fell, the new administration decided to be austere and throttle back public debt. They did not heed the advice of the Treasury mandarin, Nicholas Stern, who after writing the report on which the Act was founded stated that measures to address the problem would become progressively more expensive after 2015. They followed rather the thinking of the one-time Chancellor, Nigel Lawson, expressed in his book *An Appeal to Reason: A Cool Look at Global Warming*. Lawson's "legalistic" and contentious style wooed many who stood to lose influence from the opposite approach. His Global Warming Policy Foundation, funded by large private anonymous donations, attracted some famous emeritus professors of great age and some professors attached to Australian iron and coal production. The unfortunate politicising of the problem was not helped by Naomi Klein's impassioned left-wing book *This Changes Everything: Capitalism vs The Climate*.

54 Life Goes On?

Whether or not climate change is a myth, day-to-day life continued for ordinary people: babies were born, young people had weddings, and old people died. Not that births, marriages and deaths never change. They certainly do. Britain in the new millennium saw fewer births in the indigenous population; partnerships were often between people of the same sex, and elderly people died at an even older old age. Immigrants added to the population and filled many of the jobs that needed to be done, whether skilled or not.

But some people did die young, including our lovely Carlina. She had been a beautiful little girl with a lilt in her voice and a sense of humour. Our friends loved meeting her in the streets near us, and she loved to dance. But puberty came suddenly on her thirteenth birthday, and in the following year she lost two dear grandmothers and we moved house, away from her dream house, Moberly's, with its spacious lawn and walled kitchen garden. She lost her sparkle even if it did reappear from time to time. She wasn't helped later in her teens by the suicide of two of our friends and when she went to board at Bedales School for two years to finish her secondary education, in her very first week a boy hanged himself. A month later she suffered a psychological collapse. She recovered quickly, but it was the first of several later on.

She was an intelligent girl, going to University College, London where she read Italian and French, but she was slightly aloof, using her secretarial skills to find the money to share a flat in Fulham and live rather better than most undergraduates. This was partly due to Henry who she had met and dated while she was still at Bedales. She spent her third university year abroad just after Felicity and I separated: two months in Venice which she fell in love with, and two in Milan gaining work experience with Pirelli and living with a Pirelli family that she had known from primary school in Winchester. After that she went skiing with Henry who proposed to her in the old-fashioned way, and she accepted. Paris was the next stop where she spent three months, studying at the Sorbonne. But her time there posed all sorts of problems: difficulties in sharing a flat, difficulties with the landlord, and worries about being engaged. It was not a good time. Determined to put that right during the summer vacation she borrowed the flat in Paris belonging to our friend Nicole Genet, and spent August there.

One afternoon she telephoned me sounding very odd. She telephoned Felicity who also thought she sounded odd. Soon it became clear that she was having an attack of paranoia. Borrowing Felicity's car in the evening, I raced into Paris in the gathering gloom and was relieved when a brick aimed from an overhead bridge hit the bonnet and not the windshield. I arrived at Nicole's flat at one in the morning, got Carlina into the car, and raced away again to Calais where we caught the dawn ferry. There was fog on the M25, Carlina was asleep and my eyes kept wanting to shut. But we made it safely back to Winchester.

Once again after medical and psychiatric attention Carlina quickly recovered. But Felicity and I were worried that an attack had now happened twice. However, she went to live with Henry in a flat that they had found together in Queen's Gardens. Henry was now a trader in the City and Carlina was entering her last year at university. She was doing remarkably well, but because of what had happened, I helped her with her essays. I knew a certain amount about Italian literature, particularly Dante and Lampedusa, and I was a practised coach in the art of writing essays. But, looking back, I wonder whether I helped her too much, depriving her of the satisfaction of having done all the work herself. But she was genuinely excited by what she was studying and it was a delight for me to share her enthusiasm. In the end she achieved a good second. Soon after, she and Henry were married by Ronnie, Joan Mary's husband, in Winchester College chapel. It was a brilliant early September day with deep shadows and the leaves on the plane trees in the College's Meads shimmering in the sunlight. Then the two of them went off to Israel for their honeymoon.

For some time Carlina had been wanting to study Law, and so on their return she went to the Law School in Lancaster Gate. But the pity of it was that she started the course ten days too late, never caught up, and that was the beginning of more psychotic episodes. She was not helped by a certain lack of compatibility in her marriage. Henry loved sport, tennis in particular. He was also good at "gambling", which suited his work in the City, but he tended to carry it on into the night away from the flat. Carlina loved opera, the theatre, and travelling – frequently by herself, funded generously by Henry. But she was often alone of an evening struggling with the Law for yet another year. She began to drink, and to drink too much. That made the psychotic episodes worse, which were then treated in St. Mary's Hospital, Paddington. She recovered by doing voluntary work, and then by being paid for journalistic stints with her local newspaper. Finally, helped by Henry, she landed a good job in reporting the market for metals. Despite that, the marriage continued to deteriorate and after ten years they divorced, not without rancour.

In their marriage Henry was generous with the money he earned. But on her own Carlina spent unwisely and soon found herself under economic pressure. She had left the Metals Market and started a new and better job at the time of her divorce. The timing was bad and as a result holding down a job was difficult for her. She still travelled, when she could – to Greece, the USA, Hungary, and France. Particularly enjoyed was the week she spent alone on the Greek island of Kythera. She longed for me to share it with her. "Dad, you must go to Kythera!" she said on several occasions. But for a time her desire to drink took over and travel was out of the question. She had accidents on her moped, knocking out her teeth and damaging her leg so badly that she spent time in hospital to have a graft to cover the gaping wound. But she did eventually come to her senses. She stopped drinking, ate more wisely, lost weight without losing too much, and drank water. After a year on the new regime, Felicity and I thought it possible for us both to be out of the country in

Italy at the same time. Soon after Felicity's arrival at Macina she had a telephone conversation with Carlina from the telephone box in Civitella. And then neither of us could contact her. The silence lasted three days. We asked Natasha, Jane's eldest daughter, to visit her and find out what was happening. What she found by looking through Carlina's picture window was Carlina, lying half-dressed dead on the floor. We rushed back to Winchester, hardly knowing what we were doing. Then came the little funeral and the coroner's court. Suicide was ruled out, which gave us a very minor sense of relief. Otherwise, the cause was unknown. The most likely one, according to our medical friends, was that her heart had given out, possibly and strangely, because she had over the year drunk a great deal of water.

55 Life Continues

"Count no man happy till he's dead" was a maxim in Ancient Greece. Europe's first historian, Herodotus of Halicarnassus, illustrated it very early in his history when he told the story of Croesus, the richest man alive, entertaining Solon, the wisest man. Croesus had his chamberlain show Solon all the treasure chambers in his palace, all the gold and silver tableware, candlesticks and furniture, not to mention all the gold and silver coins, and then he asked Solon who he thought was the happiest man on Earth, expecting Solon to say: "Why, of course, Sire, it is you!" But no, Solon was having none of it. Instead he chose an obscure Athenian named Tellus who had died gloriously in battle, having witnessed all his sons and daughters living on to produce all their sons and daughters, all of whom were still alive when he died. Losing a child does not make one happy, perhaps especially if the child herself has not enjoyed the happiness that she might have had. A number of my friends have lost children. It is more common than one thinks.

But life needs to continue. At the time of Carlina's death I was involved in two projects. I was on the committee of Winchester Studies, the archaeological series on Winchester that Professor Martin Biddle edited. Martin managed his committee with great charm and he had many friends and supporters. He and his wife Birthe had very sportingly stayed in both our simple houses in Italy and had cut quite a dash with our friends in Sermugnano. Several volumes in his series had been published to considerable acclaim including the volume on the schools' dig at Lankhills. But there was a difficulty. Martin, it seemed, had a problem finishing the volumes for which he had a great deal of input. He was always very busy and the volumes always needed just a bit more. This was particularly true of a huge volume on the Anglo-Saxon Minsters, which had preceded the present Norman cathedral. The excavations had been completed in 1971; the material was supposedly ready for publication in 1997, but still nothing had been done by 2009. In addition money had run out. What was worse, Birthe, who had played a large part in the work, had sadly died in 2008. Since I had had some experience of raising money, I was engaged in that very activity partly because it was needed for another volume, *The People of Early Winchester,* some of which dealt with the skeletal remains found at Lankhills. In between the formal meetings more informal meetings were held at our house and presided over by the chairman, Barbara Bryant.

The other project was Winchester Action on Climate Change, started by another charismatic character, Robert Hutchison, who had recently retired as Chief Executive of Southern Arts and for a brief period ran Oxford's bid to be

Europe's City of Culture in 2006. I was asked by mutual friends to take part in this venture, which was inaugurated at about the same time as the passing of the Climate Change Act. Because of my earlier experience as a chairman on Winchester City Council I volunteered to chair a sub-committee on traffic and transport. These meetings were also held at our house.

Carlina's death a year later weighed heavily on me. I was sad and the sadness sapped my energy. There was also a problem about her non-existent will. For an old acquaintance of ours, who had befriended Carlina in London, insisted that Carlina had indeed made her will and had left all her possessions, including her flat, to her.

The upshot of all this was that I decided to relinquish one of the two projects with which I was involved. It seemed to me that I was more needed by Winchester Studies than by Winchester Action on Climate Change, which was developing a very healthy head of steam. It had an active and knowledgeable scientific group, a quasi-non-party-political arm, and a great many active citizens of Winchester who were well informed on environmental matters and climate change. I was, of course, still interested and kept myself up to date, both with WinACC's activities which they shared through bi-monthly open meetings, and with the wider world of the Climate Change Committee and the push-back against action by the Conservative wing of the Coalition Government.

Progress on the Winchester Studies was inching forwards. Winchester's ninth-century saint, St. Swithun, is famous for his effect on summer weather; if it rains on his saint's day, July 15, it will rain every day for another month. Little is known about him, but in 2003 Michael Lapidge produced *The Cult of St. Swithun,* a very scholarly work on the little that is known. In 2012 Yvonne Harvey's *The Winchester Mint* was published, describing and illustrating all the coins minted in the Anglo-Saxon capital, a real *tour de force*. During this period I was trying to raise money, using the lure of the "imminent" publication of *The Anglo-Saxon Minsters*. We did raise twenty-odd thousand pounds including significant donations from Winchester College and Giles Clarke. And that did help to fund the publication of *The People of Early Winchester* by Caroline Stuckert, which appeared in 2017. But the important archaeological volumes were still not in a finished state. And so I came off the committee, feeling somewhat relieved that fundraising had been taken over by wealthier people than me, with connections to the Hampshire County Council.

56. Future Generations, 2011

(Population – 7 billion; CO2 ppm – 390; Centigrade – + 1.1)

Soon after Carlina's sad and lonely death, Alessia met Adam. And a year later Otto was waiting to be born, which actually happened an hour after the summer solstice. Otto had an adventurous early life, taken first by his mother to Berlin for a quick holiday with his grandmother and great-aunt. Then six months later Alessia and Adam (and Otto) went to explore the Pyrenees to discover whether they wanted to live the good life there. Before they left, they visited Winchester. During the visit I could not help thinking that there was something odd in Alessia's manner. She was as lovely as ever, but she had changed. Not long afterwards we drove to Italy. While we were there, Alessia phoned to arrange a meeting near Mirepoix on our journey back. Then she said, "I want to tell you, Dad…"

"I know," I said. "You're pregnant!"

"That's rotten of you. How do you know? I haven't told anyone!"

"Well… There was something about you when you were in Winchester…" So we arranged to meet in the little village of Nailloux not far from the motorway between Carcasonne and Toulouse where there was a highly recommended simple restaurant.

It was a lovely little restaurant, especially lovely on a warm May midday. The village mayor and his entourage were also there; and amid much mirth and laughter Otto made eyes at the girls as only small almost-toddlers can. The girls giggled even more when he crawled over to them and tried to climb onto a lap. He was a real little boy.

Alessia had always been adventurous. She had climbed the mountains of Glencoe with an ice axe and pitons on snowy winter days when she was at university in Edinburgh. She had evacuated herself from Dharamsala, trudging through fields in the rain before the monsoons started in earnest. She was intellectually adventurous too, with four academic courses to her name (eternal student might have been a description of her): Islam with Hinduism, Environmental and Development Studies, Art, and Art Therapy in that order. And when I helped her with my pension to buy a house in Bristol, she did it up herself, including the plumbing and the electrics. As for her children, she was glad that she had had two before she was forty. Minna was the second; emotionally aware, one might say, while Otto was, and is, active and curious-minded. A practical family the four of them: Adam at the time of writing is much involved with business deals concerned with hydrogen power, beloved for the moment by the government and the international Danish shipping company, A.P. Moller-Maersk, while Alessia is a practising art therapist at a comprehensive school, having worked for Sustrans and the advertising firm, The Big Green Door. Between us, Jane and I have five grandsons and finally one granddaughter, in fact the future generation, facing Who knows What?

Otto and Rafa, the son of Lucy, Jane's second daughter, are more interested in the past than the future, the past of some 2 billion years ago when dinosaurs roamed the planet. Otto reconstructs them out of Lego; Rafa is into fossils. When he comes with his mother to England from Portugal, where Lucy and Kat, her younger sister, live with their respective partners, off we go to Lyme Regis to find fossils. There on the Jurassic coast the world of dinosaurs comes alive, so many hundreds of thousand years ago, long before any humans moved across the planet.

57 Donald Trump and the Return of Commodus, 2016

The year 2016 was eventful. In June the United Kingdom voted to leave the European Union. In July Jane and I succeeded in selling our house in Sermugnano and because of the state of European affairs were lucky to do so. In August big earthquakes rocked Umbria on the other side of the Tiber Valley and destroyed houses, lives, and livelihoods. In November Mr. Trump was elected Mr. President of the United States of America. 2016 was also the hottest year for the whole globe since records began.

The vote for Brexit was disastrous, not necessarily for the actual decision, which might in the end prove to be good, but for the schisms and weaknesses that it showed up in the processes of the British government. To me the Brexiteers seemed mostly a shifty lot, giving the impression of being out for their own ends; the Conservative leadership was too smug and too wrongly aligned in European politics properly to argue the case for remaining in the European Union. The opposition parties were weak and trivial. The whole thing was a shambles.

What happened in the United Kingdom was more than equalled for its awfulness by the United States. If the narcissistic Mr. Johnson, one of the architects for Brexit, liked being loved for his popular image rather than for whatever course of action he chose to patronise, Mr. Trump's narcissism, glorying in the adoring echoes he heard from his supporters, was in a different league. He thrived on a violence of oratory that was totally self-centred. He was like the Roman Emperor Commodus who actually performed for his admirers as a gladiator on the arena in the Colosseum. And like Commodus he symbolised the end of a period of unparalleled affluence and apparent progress in the Western World. Commodus was assassinated and deserved his fate, but the Decline of the Roman Empire, though slow, was inexorable, as Edward Gibbon related in his famous book.

Our departure from Sermugnano was a very personal event, attended by a sadness that was wider than just moving house. We had arrived from England on our last but one visit to find our dear friend Lillo stretched out dying on his bed, with his mouth open, just alive enough for us to whisper our goodbyes in his ear. Family members and a number of villagers were sitting quietly around the room waiting for him finally to go. By the time we came back the next day his spirit had left him. His body was still in the same place, now dressed in his Sunday best, his feet in fine slippers adorned with red ribbons and a bandage round his chin to keep his mouth in place. The funeral was on that day – so soon after his death. He was put in a simple coffin upstairs in his bedroom. The coffin was then taken laboriously down three flights of stairs, manoeuvred out through the front door at an angle and taken across the corner of the piazza to the church just twenty yards away. The service started soon afterwards. The young mayor of Castiglione was present, as was the local head of Opus Dei, who thought very well of himself. Augusto was there too without any airs or graces even though he had been one of the most influential men in Italy. All the women of the village were there. Most of the men stood waiting and chatting outside in the piazza until it was time to join the funeral procession to the cemetery. They had to wait some time because the priest went on, long and low, with us hearing little and understanding less. Then we trailed up to the cemetery, with the coffin and coffin-bearers some way ahead of us.

We had never been to an Italian funeral. We waited like the others in the little built-up cemetery with the grander family tombs on the periphery and the less grand in a sort of tenement block in the middle, divided into pigeon-holes on four levels. The crowd began to stir when a hand appeared out of Lillo's pigeon-hole: a rather bizarre manifestation we thought. But clearly it was part of a normal procedure: somebody had to cement in the coffin. And that was that. There was no wake, and we all trailed back to the village, each to our own.

We had come to know Franca and Giuliano well. They had joined up with Lillo and Gabriela sometimes to eat and drink with us of an evening, sitting on our upper terrace. Then the evening shadows would climb up the Umbrian mountains and soon the moon, often full (or so it seemed), would appear, sliding slowly above the mountain ridge. It was about that time of an evening that a man with a very upright bearing used to walk past the house, having ascended, we presumed, the rough and crumbly, dangerous path from down below. At a certain point towards the end of our time he ceased to come. And so we asked Franca who he was, this distinguished-looking man, who always gave us a grave but friendly "Buona sera!" To our surprise, she said it was her father. He had died at some point while we were in Winchester. But what he had been doing was spending time during the day in the orchards and small fields where once he and his wife and only child had eked out their living. "Eked" is not exactly the right word. Franca's memory of it was of a time of comparative but simple plenty. The only thing she disliked was the necessity of going to the school in the village, walking up and down that precipitous path every day. "Would you like to see our old house?" she asked. "We would love to," we replied.

And so, one day, soon after, we climbed into Giuliano's car to go round the spur of the hill on which Sermugnano stands, thus avoiding a potentially fatal fall down the precipitous path. We went first to the site of the Etruscan town at the very end of the spur where archaeologists from Rome had been spending the summer uncovering the remains. There was little to see, because the trenches had been filled in for the winter, but the story was that they had found what must have been an important town in its heyday before the Romans took a grip on the area. From there we descended to Franca's home. Her house for a time had been abandoned, but had eventually been bought by the incomer from Opus Dei and rented out. When we saw it, a Japanese lady occupied it from time to time. On that day the beautiful old house was empty. It was not as tall as Macina, but longer and bigger, roofed over with the usual curved "canale" tiles, its walls constructed with well-cut tufa blocks. Unlike Macina, which was on a steep hillside, this house was surrounded, but not hemmed in, by large chestnut trees and through them we could see an open orchard of walnut and olive trees with a small vineyard up an incline beyond. The grounds were half abandoned but a relative of Franca was looking after the olives and walnuts. Slightly down from them a small stream flowed, which never came close to drying out but provided water all year round both for the house and for one of those wonderful, open stone troughs where they washed all their laundry, cool in the shade of a chestnut tree. Franca was clearly in love with her old home and felt that her life had not been improved by going up into the little town. We were much moved that she had shown it to us.

Our last visit to Sermugnano came not long after. The ownership of our house went to an English couple from Bishop Auckland and the deed was done in the dingy office of the notary in Bagnoregio. The process was interminable. All the documents had to be read out in Italian and repeated in English, because, literacy, as we knew, is still not an accomplishment of every Italian. We went back to the house to collect such belongings as we were taking home. But as a final act I decided to have a quick look at the excavations, which on this occasion did coincide with our visit. But there had been torrential rain the previous night and no one was there. Instead, I went down a small wooded path on the side of the hill to a point where on our expedition to Franca's house we thought we had seen in the steep face of the hill the outline of a gateway. But the rain had swept down the path and the hillside had collapsed. What I did see in the water-scoured surface of the path was a perfect black roundel, some two feet wide, just edging out of the ground. What could it be? Only one thing came to mind: an Etruscan funerary vessel in black bucchero ware sliced off in the middle with the bottom half still under the ground.

58 Family and Friends

Our departure from Italy was bound to bring great change to our lives. Our one base was now in Winchester and the UK. No longer would we be paying taxes in Castiglione and making sure that our house was watertight and in good order. We would need to concentrate on doing that sort of thing in our small terraced house before we became too decrepit to care. After all we were not going to live for ever. It was the time of life, too, when we would be saying goodbye to more friends like Lillo. This quickly proved only too true. For soon after our arrival back in England, my cousin Alison, the unlikely laird of Finzean, suddenly died. She and her husband Angus had been wonderful occupants of that estate, with its river, fields, forests, hills and heather-clad mountains. They had encouraged people to stay in the village, making sure that there was enough small industry to provide work and enough houses to prevent the school ever lacking children. They made sure that the Scots pine forest was reseeded naturally to be a home for capercailzie, red squirrels and pine martins. People coming from Aberdeen and elsewhere for a day's outing had plenty of paths to walk on and spaces to enjoy. Angus became the lord lieutenant of the county; and at the time of one of the Queen's most difficult years, between them, Angus and Alison were in a position to give her their gift of sympathetic and understanding attention. Alison was buried in the new village graveyard on the side of the hill near the kirk. Many people gathered round, cold in the grey north wind, and Archie, one of her grandsons, played the pipes. When the coffin was lowered the sun came out and stayed out until a great many people came back to the big house for the wake.

My sister too, JM, had for some time been in great pain

from her back and right leg, a condition which seemed to stem from that minor attack, possibly of polio, that she had sustained so long ago in Assam. She was now a widow with four grown-up children strung across the globe from New Jersey to Vietnam. She had lived in the house which she and Ronnie had bought for their retirement after they had left their Herefordshire vicarage. Then it had all become too difficult and she went to a care home found by her eldest daughter who had returned from her time as a midwife in the Shetlands. JM had been a great walker and sailor but now she was confined to her room and then to her bed. I visited her regularly, often with Jane, and we had good laughs about our parents and our times in India and East Lothian, and I learnt more about her life than I had ever known before. She was a staunch Christian, tried very lightly to persuade me to believe in the resurrection of the dead and the after-life, but eventually sailed off herself into the sunset.

COMING TO THE STARTING LINE, 2015–2021

59 From COP21 towards COP26

To all those who could see a huge turbulence on the horizon unless positive steps were taken not to succumb to it but to use it, the December 2015 Climate Change Conference (COP21) in Paris brought relief and hope. One hundred and ninety four nations had signed up to take steps on their own account to avoid what, they agreed, was a climate catastrophe unless the rise in the world temperature since Victorian times was limited to 2 degrees Celsius (changed later to 1.5 degrees). It would not be just humans that suffered but the whole of nature as we know it: water, air, and soil, plankton, plants, and insects, wild animals, domestic animals, and Man. For Man would suffer horribly if everything else were to be severely diminished. Nor was it just temperature that was the problem, but human products such as plastic and the sheer waste and detritus with which humans are defiling the world.

But in the United Kingdom there was a difficulty. The Conservative part of the Coalition government gave the impression of being only mildly interested in global warming, and Liberal Democrat politicians were once again committing political suicide: the Secretary of State for the Environment, the Liberal Democrat Chris Huhne, was caught lying about a driving offence and found himself in prison. The Conservative prime minister took advantage of his absence and (despite an early promise on climate change and riding a bike to work) not only pulled out of giving support to the manufacture of wind turbines and solar panels but also passed legislation making it more difficult to deploy these structures on dry land.

The Conservatives did, however, once free of the coalition, agree to the Paris Accord.

Agreement was one thing, action another. Brexit was focussing attention and Brexiteers were too intent on their mission to think about climate change. Party politics also got in the way. A new centre-right government was not impressed with the likes of Naomi Klein and the fact that it was a centre-left administration that brought in the Climate Change Act of 2008. To someone like me, who quite by chance of nature, nurture and environment had been aware of what was going on, dimly to begin with and then more and more clearly, the inaction was extraordinarily frustrating. Most people of my acquaintance did not want to begin to think about it. Or if they did begin, they only reached the point of dismissing it with a joke or the legalistic arguments of a Nigel Lawson, taking no account of the science except to draw attention to sceptics. It may be that few people understand science in their adult years except as a means of creating items, whether soap, cars, or space rockets, to render human life more comfortable or more replete with marvels.

Whatever the case, it was so frustrating that I decided to go to a counsellor, mostly to let off some steam and talk about my own difficulties of communication, but also because I recognised that the dysfunction between words and action could affect the psychological well-being of others. I chose a counsellor with an understanding of history who lived in Southampton. Unfortunately she left me even more frustrated. After I had given her an idea of my life as well as the immediate problem, she chose to concentrate on the loss of my daughter. Though I was sad whenever I talked about Carlina's death, I had come to terms with her loss. But the counsellor would not let up. I received the impression that this was her "safe zone", and so when she asked me to come back for a second session, I politely declined.

I had in the meantime begun to go to more meetings of WinACC. Its founder, Robert Hutchison, was not now so involved. He was one of those people who are extraordinarily good at starting projects, but then leave them for other people to pursue. He had a passion for poetry which he indulged to the full by forming a Winchester poetry society. He also became a Liberal Democrat City Councillor, thus making it even clearer that action on climate change was not a Conservative concern, even if the Conservative-controlled district council paid lip service to it. WinACC, for its part, was being very ably run by its energetic and passionate director, Christine Holloway, who had gained wide experience in both public and private domains. It was a seed bed of good ideas, backed up by evidence, but it was difficult to widen its influence.

I still continued to read relevant books by authors who endorsed and amplified the climate science, and also by sceptics like Bjorn Lomborg, the French engineer Christian Gerondeau, and articles published by Nigel Lawson's Global Warming Policy Foundation. For a long time, as described earlier, I had regarded James Martin, the author of *The Meaning of the 21st Century* as particularly cogent amongst those who regarded climate change as our most pressing threat. His famous canyon was now much closer. But his optimistic view, as an early practitioner of information technology, that IT would give us the means to come out of the canyon bruised but not broken, was being questioned. The Israeli polymath, Yuval Noah Harare, saw it as yet another threat, not an opportunity. In his book *Homo Deus* he foresaw a world in which there was so much expanding information that it would become increasingly difficult to select what was relevant and discard the irrelevant, not to mention the rapidly increasing danger of fake news and malware. He agreed that climate change was the fundamental danger and placed beside it artificial intelligence. This pessimistic outlook was compounded by a mammoth volume entitled *Global Crisis: Wars, Climate Change, and Catastrophe in the Seventeenth Century* by the historian Geoffrey Parker. Its subject was the century-long cold weather experienced in the Northern Hemisphere, sometimes called the Maunder Minimum. His basic thesis was that climate change causes political and social chaos.

60 Action Stations, Chairing Winchester Action on Climate Change, 2018–2020

In the first week of October 2018 the International Panel on Climate Change (IPCC) met at Incheon in South Korea for its COP23 and reassessed the global temperature for 2050. It came to the conclusion that, instead of limiting the temperature rise to 2 degrees Celsius above its level at the beginning of the Industrial Revolution, it should be 1.5 degrees. It also decided that unless the process had begun in earnest by 2030, the situation would become catastrophic.

The most obvious public reaction to this unwelcome news was Greta Thunberg's, the now famous, autistic fifteen-year-old schoolgirl from Stockholm. But within the month those with deeper knowledge were truly alarmed. At the beginning of November I attended the Annual General Meeting of Winchester Action on Climate Change. AGMs are never likely to shake the Earth, and this one didn't; WinACC was just getting on with the job. Its members, however, knew the score on climate change. But I was alarmed that the organisation's excellent chair, Tony Stoller CBE, who had not been well, had resigned three months previously and no successor had yet been found. It happened that I had only just finished the rather unsatisfactory first draft of this book, containing as it did too much data, and I was at the point of trying to remedy the problem, fully intending to finish another draft and hoping eventually to publish it. But it struck me at the AGM that this book could wait. It was much more important to keep WinACC moving. And so I put my name forward for the position of chair. In any case the world never stops turning, and such a book as I was likely to finish would not be readable if it concentrated too closely on facts and figures.

Four months passed and I heard nothing from WinACC. Eventually I pushed hard, asked for an interview, and got it. The interview was well put together and I thought that I had performed satisfactorily. The final question was "What would your first action be?" This was not difficult for a candidate now past his eightieth birthday. "Find my successor!" was my answer. And so for the next eighteen months I chaired WinACC.

It was not an easy task. Christine Holloway had retired as director almost two years earlier, but the change to a new director had been difficult, not least because there was no forward movement nationally and the local government administrations in Hampshire and Winchester were becalmed and hurt by ongoing austerity. The first crisis I encountered (let alone my first action) was the resignation of the director. He resigned very gracefully and the only problem he caused was that, the finances of the organisation being what they were, I was constrained to take on some of the burdens of a director. As often with charitable organisations, the volunteers, passionate about the subject and well-versed in their own fields, were not always an easy fit. But I was more concerned about my own technical shortcomings. I had not used the full possibilities of computing for eighteen years and I had a great deal to learn, with not much time to do so within everything else; what took others ten minutes took me half an hour. This was especially irksome once Covid-19 had struck and most work had to be done remotely. My fellow volunteers were very patient and I was in the organisation long enough for its problems to settle down and be resolved. An excellent communications manager was found and an excellent company secretary. Christine Holloway took over as chair just for one year and a good team was ready for the future. And so, I was able to bow out, reasonably satisfied that my presence had been of some use. During that time, without much help from me, WinACC had engaged with both the district and county councils, and had influenced each of them sufficiently (one Liberal Democrat, the other Conservative) for them to declare a climate crisis and start rearranging their budgets accordingly.

It was then that I came to writing the second draft of this book in the third wave of the pandemic. But circumstances had radically changed. In the first draft I was trying to show how and why the world as we knew it was coming to an end; for this second draft we have already entered James Martin's canyon and our little boat, bouncing around on the rapids, is beset by plague. From this book's point of view at least, I don't have to use too much data. For it was data and the "inconvenience" of the truth that put many off considering the implications of climate change. Now, however, there was hope that the powers-that-be would begin to take notice.

61 A Diversion in the Time of Plague, 2020

In the first wave of Covid-19 the spring sun shone day in day out. It was so strong that it hurt my eyes. We could easily have been in Italy; which reminded me of a house party attended by ten citizens of Florence, seven rich young women and three rich young men, who had escaped to the hilltop town of Fiesole, for the year was 1348 and the pandemic of the Black Death had struck. Boccaccio in his *Decameron* imagines them passing their voluntary lockdown recounting amusing stories to each other. Our very own Chaucer in his *Canterbury Tales* picked up the theme of story-telling. But whereas Chaucer's characters were a patchwork bunch, Boccaccio's were all well-to-do and mostly oblivious to the pain and carnage that the plague was wreaking amongst the many slaves, servants, and artisans who had been left behind in the fetid atmosphere of Florence, at the bottom of the hill.

Jane and I, like many in Winchester, felt lucky that we had our little, south-facing garden which we could cultivate and enjoy. It was peaceful: the wrens, chaffinches and blackbirds sang, and our air was free of the usual sound and smell of traffic. We were, though, aware from the media that many people were stuck in small city flats, squashed together in high-rise buildings, some of them crumbling, damp, and in great need of repair; nurses, doctors and carers, too, were slaving away in dangerous and crowded conditions. At our age there was not a great deal we could do. Our kind neighbours actually offered us help; but Jane, until her back gave out, spent some time helping at Home Start and I was deep in the data and complexities of WinACC. But then ten months later, in the third wave of the pandemic, when people on the front line were feeling drained and many families were under stress with parents and children all working at home, I went back to writing this book. But like the well-to-do young people in 1348, I took the opportunity for a small diversion, to the time when some fifty years ago the seed of an idea drifted into my mind.

I had been reading a seminal book by Professor W. K. C. Guthrie, entitled *The Greeks and their Gods*. Its central question was: How could Zeus, the King of the Gods and Lord of the Heavens, also have been born as a little baby boy in a cave near the top of Mt. Dikte in Crete? And once born how could such an august figure have been fed by bees and when he cried, be protected from his baby-eating father by dancers clashing cymbals to drown out his baby noises? The answer is Great Zeus was a synthesis of two characters, the Lord of the Skies and the baby god born of a powerful goddess. The Lord of the Skies was the great god of nomadic tribes riding their horses over the vast steppes of the North and under limitless heavens before arriving in the Mediterranean. There they encountered and conquered agricultural people living in deep, mountain-bound valleys who believed in the fertility of the soil. Their most powerful deities were goddesses who gave birth to baby boys. Zeus, or Father Zeus, Zeus Pater as he was often called in Ancient Greece, can be found in Italy as Jupiter or in Northern India as DyausPitar. The nomads clearly got around. Yahweh, the Hebrew god was also the god of desert nomads. Less mobile were the goddesses because they were linked to their own plots of land, whether Athene in Athens, Hera in Argos, Osiris in Egypt or Ishtar in Mesopotamia. When reading Professor Guthrie many years ago, I thought that this pattern was not irrelevant to our modern world.

For whereas in the Ancient World there was room enough and to spare for nomads to gallop around invading territory, in the modern world the globe is filling up and soon, I thought, there would be no more half-empty habitable spaces. So what could happen? Would the nations not have to come together and agree on how to manage the small space they had in common? Could this not be a common danger that brings individuals and nations to work together, without any significant war and aggression? Would it not be the female of the species who by nature would be playing a leading part to guard the productivity of the land and safety of the household? Unfortunately, for at least 6,000 years the male-led nomads have held sway, and it is no coincidence that starting with the Father of History, the Greek Herodotus, the most popular subject for historians and epic poetry has until recently been… WAR. But perhaps it is not a coincidence either that women are slowly becoming more and more prominent in public matters and more histories are written about domestic and personal matters. Such changes do not come readily. Men can easily resent a competing power in the management of things, resulting in violence and abuse, both physical and verbal. Women, too, can become more male than men in order to assert their role in the management of things. This is where we are now. But in my view the direction is clear.

The pandemic itself illustrates these lessons. Born

possibly of a natural, non-human source, whether bats or pangolins, and whether it is indeed the start of James Lovelock's Revenge of Gaia, it permeates the whole globe, necessitating the cooperation of all humanity and the emotional and practical human resources seen particularly in women. In essence the pandemic is the first lesson in an extended course of learning that we humans will be taking up, I hope, to make our house habitable for the future. It is, however, not yet agreed that the rich nations, for their very own safety as well as for moral humanitarian reasons, must help poor nations with their supply of vaccine to prevent the pandemic, like a forest fire, from blazing up once again in untended places.

62 An Interlude with the Pope

Pope Francis also allowed himself a little time during the pandemic to write a book. He is environmentally aware, as his adopted name suggests. He is, however, not a Franciscan, but a scientific Jesuit. He is also able to plot the direction humanity is taking within a context of 4,000 years of biblical history. In his book, *Let Us Dream,* he regards the pandemic as a wake-up call to everyone, a call to change our mindsets. The old-fashioned word for that is "Repent!" To me the word "repent" sounds too punitive and linked to guilt; "changing one's mindset" is closer to the original Greek of the New Testament. Nevertheless, "Repent" has a useful, necessary, sharp quality in this situation. The Pope also uses the word "dream", I suspect, in its deepest meaning of "thoughts closest to one's heart". The Roman Catholic Church has often been far from admirable, whether one thinks of the Borgias in the sixteenth century, of its recent sexual abuses in Ireland or pecuniary corruption in the Vatican itself. But I cannot help admiring this man in his regard for the value of humanity as a whole, including people of faiths different from his, like the Rohingyas, Uighurs, and Iraqi Shiites. He also has a high regard for women, women economists like Mariana Mazzucato and Kate Raworth, who think Value is a more important yardstick in economics than Growth which nowadays is so fixated on Numbers and Wealth – wealth just for its own sake.

In her *The Value of Everything: Making and Taking in the Global Economy* Mazzucato traces the present practice of economists back to, and further back from, Adam Smith, to the present day and what she calls The Rise in Casino Capitalism, by which huge wealth is amassed by only a very few people, is then stacked away in off-shore tax havens, and as a result of the whole process has little real value for the problems that the globe faces.

Kate Raworth, a top graduate of Oxford University's school of Politics, Philosophy and Economics, similarly in her *Doughnut Economics* believes that PPE has taken a wrong turn towards uselessness in its application to the real world. I am not a trained economist, but as a "div don" at Winchester College I needed to have some understanding of it and just wish that these two women (and, I believe, other female economists) were educating people thirty years ago.

The Pope comes as near as a pope can to saying that women are as well-endowed as men with practical holy qualities. The original St. Francis was not of that mind. He made his faithful follower, St. Clare, go into a nunnery from where she was not allowed to emerge, nor was she given licence to speak to anyone (except in the novel that I had written during my sabbatical).

63 Amid James Martin's Canyon, 2021

The pandemic that is now engulfing all humanity can be viewed as the first, very testing, rapid water rushing down James Martin's canyon. The pandemic is amplifying conditions on the globe that are already difficult. The chaos is not in any way like the hardships faced by a large proportion of the billion or so humans who lived before 1800. In those days human settlements were relatively far apart from each other and news travelled slowly. Now that there are 8 billion of us, we are so close to each other in space and time that collisions can scarcely be avoided, whether they are about territory, history, ideas, gender and racial identities, or power, whether at an individual or national level. More recently it was easier in the days when there were blocs: communism and capitalism, with or without fascism. Such blocs struggled against each other to extend their power amongst the unaligned, but (for better or worse – and it could be very bad) the conflicts had a clearer definition, whether in the two World Wars, the Cold War, Korea or Vietnam. Now even in an era of world trade we know of many dissociated internal or external conflicts: for instance the UK seems to be in the throes of breaking up, the EU too, the USA is hugely divided, Russia is ruled by an ex-KGB mafioso intent on extending his power, China is belligerent and seems to be indulging in ethnic cleansing, Syria has imploded, Myanmar is imploding, Ethiopia is imploding (again), so too is Columbia (again) and the old splits between Sunnis and Shiites, Muslims and Hindus are opening up. It is even possible that the Taliban will kick the USA and its NATO allies out of Afghanistan, much to the delight of would-be terrorists, and much to the detriment of the advance of women. And I am not mentioning the Yemen, Byelorussia and many other countries. All this is exacerbated by the explosion of knowledge, fake news, instant, un-thought-out reactions and cyber warfare.

As for hope, some does exist in these dangerous days. The very speed of intercommunication could have the power to pull humanity together, particularly with common danger in sight. At the time of writing, the world has thirty years to reach the position of having unambiguously delineated and resolved the crisis. The first climate change conference, held in Rio, was twenty-nine years ago, and so we are halfway through our time for change, wasted years according to Sir Dieter Helm, the highly acclaimed economist and energy expert. The knowledge is, however, now right out in the open. Yet – it can easily be missed by intelligent people whose backgrounds have often been too focussed on their particular interests and professions. But it is ready for leaders who can learn from the past and guide the process through the next series of rapids in the canyon caused by the warming world under its atmospheric blanket of carbon dioxide.

At the moment there are few leaders who show much knowledge about climate change. And many leaders on the international stage have dubious credentials. Think Putin and Bolsonaro for a start. But the change from Trump to Biden is one source of hope, despite the divisions in the USA. The dark horse, in every respect, is Xi Jing Ping, the new Great Leader of China. Unfortunately, the secrecy of his autocratic government, particularly on the origins of the pandemic, does not inspire in people that vital base for action; trust. And like Putin he is flexing his muscles at a particularly unfortunate time.

64 Preparing for COP26: Boris and Rishi, 2021

The Climate Change Conference (COP26) in Glasgow during November 2021 is regarded as the necessary turning point in mankind's struggle to eliminate human habits that are so destructive to Planet Earth, our one and only home. The UK is the host nation at the conference but the really important players will prove to be the USA and China, particularly the USA with its Climate Change Envoy, John Kerry, crossing and recrossing the planet in search of consensus. In the UK there are four people, all men, who are of some importance: Boris Johnson, Rishi Sunak, Alok Sharma, and Mark Carney. Of course it may happen that in the chaos of the pandemic and in the ebb and flow of political rivalries they will be replaced, or even that the conference will still not happen. It is the inhabitants, however, of Nos. 10 and 11 Downing Street, Boris and Rishi, on whom the final responsibility of events will bear down. Boris will be the political signatory for the UK; Rishi will be in charge of the UK's finances, to show the world that the UK means business. As hosts they will be setting the tone for the conference and be subject to judgement by others. The conference that they are hosting may be a success or it may be a failure, but – though vital – it is still only the starting line for a strategy to be followed for at least the next thirty years, until 2050. Luckily, perhaps, they are still quite young: Rishi, in particular will have only reached seventy in 2050, the final cut-off date for the completion of the strategy. But are they up to the task at this present time, both at the conference and for the following year when the UK will still be in charge?

There will be many people attending the conference, in person, one hopes, rather than at a zoomed-in distance. Scientists will be there, not just members of the International

Panel of Climate Change (the IPCC), but others too, as well as scientific journalists, from all over the world. Leaders of multinational companies will also be there, many of them looking for opportunities to help and at the same time to make money. Some huge companies, particularly those dealing with oil and coal, (some of them really the property of national governments as in Saudi Arabia) will be making the right noises, but in the background and out of sight might be carrying on, regardless of the cost to the Earth of their actions. These companies, it is now common knowledge, have known the science for more than thirty years but have paid it no attention for all that time. In failing to do so they have done huge damage to trust. Finally there will be many, many individuals from all over the world actually in Glasgow, or following proceedings very closely from afar.

But it is the politicians and their advisers who have to pull the strands together. And the British politicians, as hosts, are in a position of considerable responsibility. That is the main reason why I am concentrating on them. But there is also another reason: it so happens that I and my extended family have had some small personal connection with both Boris and Rishi. And, not surprisingly, each of them has been subject to an up-to-date biography; *Boris Johnson: the Gambler* by Tom Bower, and *Going for Broke; the Rise of Rishi Sunak* by Michael Ashcroft. I have read both books.

There is one more important reason. Both men were at independent boarding schools, Boris at Eton, Rishi at Winchester, schools of great renown and much expense. I have intimate knowledge of boarding schools, but as a group (particularly the male-only boarding schools) they are facing sharp attacks from a few unhappy alumni and, more importantly, psychologists, often women, who accuse them of deadening the sensitivities and flexibilities of mind of the very people who aspire to be political leaders and at the top of their professions. It is becoming more and more agreed that the earliest years of a child's life are vital for giving that child the confidence it needs through the love and security of its parents. But adolescence is the next important stage and it is argued that as a result of the wrench away from parental life and of too much constant exposure to the vagaries and banter of children, both as individuals and in a crowd, not to mention the occasional predatory teacher, psychological defences become erected which inhibit later normal and necessary mental and psychological flexibility.

I, of course, grew up in such a system, but the circumstances in which I did so, in the last days of the British Empire and just after a dreadful war, made boarding a much more acceptable choice of school. There was a wider purpose to it, when one's parents were likely to move around to a variety of different military, colonial or diplomatic postings. My parents made as sure as they could that I was prepared at the age of seven – that it was a natural thing to do. I did not feel a lack of love at home because of it. I did, however, feel homesick and certainly grew away from my parents, but I was much helped to have confidence by such abilities that I had and the fact that they were recognised. Nowadays there is not such a need for a child to board. Nevertheless, during my time of teaching at Winchester, the schools like it became more and more expensive, more and more extensive in their facilities, and more and more an education only for the wealthy who are more and more driven to push their offspring to achieve "great" things. I have come to recognise that this favours no one. It tends to limit the experience of the children to a narrow elite, and that narrow elite tends to think too much of itself and that it is born to leadership and government. Thus its psychological outlook is narrowed. Unfortunately, this "leadership" sets the tone for able people aspiring to take their place. And included amongst them will be those who are lucky enough to be awarded bursaries at these schools, despite the fact that a large majority of them are still among the top 10 per cent of the world's wealthiest people, the group whose habits and ability to consume account for at least 50 per cent of CO_2 emissions on the planet. What's more the gap between the rich and poor of the world is becoming steadily larger. As for the tone set by the alumni of boarding schools a demonstration of this could be in the House of Commons where Prime Minister's Question Time and debates too often resemble the clever, clever schoolboy debates at an Eton or Winchester.

So then, how are Boris and Rishi likely to fare in their great positions of state at a really difficult time, with a raging pandemic very much in place and the climate crisis beginning to bite? As I have said, my extended family and I myself have some personal experience of them. And it is hard not to feel sorry for them as they face a maelstrom of events which their recent predecessors could have foreseen, but from which they looked the other way.

Boris once had a close, unpremeditated encounter with my admirable, charming, just so slightly eccentric, eldest stepdaughter, Natasha. She had often seen him playing tennis on Highbury Fields near where she lives with her husband and little boy. But it was in Holborn that she really did meet him. She was walking to work. She always walks, everywhere. Anyway, she was just about to cross a road at traffic lights, looking right then left then right again, when, on turning to the right the second time, she saw a familiar figure coming up, rather dishevelled, on a bicycle. She is not one to miss a trick, especially as this figure, pulling up for the lights on his bike beside her, was Boris, the Mayor of London.

"Boris!" she said addressing him. "I belong to a boxing club in North London. I've been there for twenty years. Wouldn't it be a really good thing if boxing and ballet were taught in London's primary schools? You know, to give all that testosterone and energy a fun outlet?"

She was on a roll and suddenly realised that his hand was clasping hers. She hadn't noticed it slipping in there. Not put off at all, she continued. He released his grip and fumbled in his jacket. He was trying to find a pen or card or something. "Look," said Boris. "Speak to Kate. Kate Hoey. She's my advisor on sport. We've been working together on the Olympics. She'll be very interested!"

Then the lights turned green. Boris had missed them twice already. He hitched up his trousers, pushed on a pedal with his right foot and wobbled off. Natasha waited for the little green man to shine. Then she too went, with a spring in her step. And later that day she phoned Kate Hoey's office.

Boris going round London just chatting to people reminded me slightly of my duties as Second Master going round Winchester College to get myself properly reacquainted with it, and with its staff and pupils. Boris would have made a good teacher at a boys' independent boarding school, a much better one than me. He would have been great fun, on the ball, and would have talked the schoolboy talk. And that's what got him elected to high office. "It'll be fun to have Boris as PM!" I have heard Conservative friends say. "Yes, he was a fun mayor of London."

But more than that...? He likes, everybody says, to be loved. He makes promises, in order to be loved. And then forgets them. Whether they are promises to his wife, or partners, or in matters of state, or to a pushy captain of industry, whether on foreign aid, or on matters of transparency. It has always been difficult for him to focus on anything for long. According to his biographers, his early years of life were so insecure that he developed a self-centred carapace to protect himself, a carapace that became thicker when he was at Eton. And now because he is prime minister, it seems that he expects to know everything. And, it seems, he believes he does.

I do think, however, that he has the ability to "think outside the box". Maybe that's because he is scarcely ever in it. Unfortunately it is that character trait which makes him vulnerable to distrust, especially for leaders of governments outside the UK, and indeed in his own political party. In his earlier life he has not looked trustworthy. Yet it is that very trust which is needed to get his good ideas (from outside the box) put into action. On climate change, at a certain tipping point, everyone will need to take part – and that will be a problem without trust in our leaders.

Rishi Sunak is a very different character, but he does share a youthful ambition with Boris: from his earliest teens he too wanted to be prime minister. Does that mean that both of them in some sense stopped developing at that stage? I was Rishi's div don for a year when he was seventeen. He was extremely alert, spoke well, and had a charm that was very different from the charm Boris undoubtedly has. He didn't make enemies. As an older boy, it is clear that he was solicitous for the welfare of the younger ones. He focussed on what he thought was important, and did enough on what he thought was comparatively unimportant. He wanted to please, but not to be loved. His parents did the loving, which was not obvious in the case of Boris's father. But Rishi's medical parents, one a doctor, the other a pharmacist, were a steady influence and made sure that Rishi and his siblings did their homework, to the minute. This is not untypical of Hindu families who want to make good. There is an anecdote about a young friend who had come to play football in the garden but was told to wait outside for a full quarter of an hour until the homework was finished. Rishi was not a "boarder" at Winchester College. Coming back to the security of his ambitious parents every night makes his teenage experiences very different from those of Boris or of most children at boarding schools.

Rishi possibly taught me more than I taught him. When he was in my div, I can't remember putting the Bhagavad Gita on the syllabus I intended to teach. But I do remember him correcting my pronunciation of the Mahabharata, one of the two great Hindu epics. The Bhagavad Gita has a section to itself inside it. "Sir!" said Rishi (he was always very polite, even by Wykehamical standards). "The stress is on the middle A, not on the penultimate."

"Thank you very much, Rishi. I'll always remember that," – and I have. He was in the last div that I ever taught. I still have the book containing the marks I gave him for his fortnightly essays. When he became an MP, he took his oath of allegiance on the Bhagavad Gita, not the Bible. Not surprisingly the Gita sees hard, conscientious work as a sort of meditation.

Rishi went to Oxford University to read PPE, and duly achieved a First Class degree. Then he was awarded a Fulbright scholarship to Stanford Graduate School of Business in California, before working with Goldman Sachs and in hedge funds, in effect in Casino Capitalism. I do worry that in the pursuit of his career and the wealth to go with it, he may have hardened some innate inflexibility of mind.

Whereas Boris has been peddling around the political centres of Westminster and Brussels since early adulthood, Rishi became involved in official politics only when he stood for Parliament in 2015, having first made sure that his personal fortunes of all kinds were secure. He had become a multi-millionaire in his own right, he had married in due course a talented Indian wife, also a multi-millionaire, the daughter of a highly successful entrepreneur in information technology. Finally, through, it seems possible, friendships with Michael Ashcroft and William Hague (a previous leader of the Conservative parliamentary party) he had been put on the long list of candidates for the impregnable Tory constituency of Richmond in Yorkshire. He impressed the several selection committees to such an extent that, despite formidable local and rival candidates and being himself a novice, he was duly selected and entered Parliament in 2015. His political persona is very different from Boris's. Boris has charm but is often short of money; Rishi has charm and the spirit and means for generosity. Boris has been called "The Gambler". Rishi's mathematical mind thinks everything through and, because he has had such success gambling in Casino Capitalism, he can scarcely be called a "gambler" in the sense that that word has become attached to Boris.

One of Rishi's earliest actions while he was an MP was to write an impressive paper on the internet for the centre-right think tank, Policy Exchange, entitled *Undersea Cables: Indispensable, Insecure* published in December 2017. With his in-law's practical experience of the mechanical side of internet technology and with the written blessing of no less than an ex-Supreme Allied Commander Europe, an-ex Chief of Defence Staff UK, and an ex-Director of GCHQ, it was a shrewd choice, very successfully completed. It was a sign, amongst other things, of something quite clear from his teens, namely his unusual ability to network, and that depends on his ability to listen. I was amused when I looked at a map of the layout of the cables running under every ocean in the world and through many a narrow, vulnerable strait. Rishi had, as it were, entwined the world with tentacles full of neurons.

With his Indian background and experience of the upper echelons of India itself, not to mention his years in the USA, it is not surprising that he was a staunch backer of Brexit. He has a global instinct. Whether this instinct is the right sort of global instinct, that is to say, whether he has any true idea of the vulnerability of the globe and the vulnerability of its poorest inhabitants to human excess, or whether deep down he regards the planet as a treasure trove to be exploited and its "untouchables" as expendable, is still unfortunately a matter of conjecture.

When, early in 2020, the pandemic was migrating from its birthplace in Wuhan and was already ravaging Northern Italy, it was also spreading without as yet many alarm bells ringing across the UK. But on March 11, Rishi as an unexpectedly new Chancellor of the Exchequer gave a remarkable Budget presentation in the House of Commons. It was remarkable not only for the unprecedented slew of funds he was disbursing to help people through the widespread hardships about to be caused by the disease, but also for its carefully crafted panache. What was even more remarkable, he had been in office for less than a month and had enjoyed scarcely any time to pull his speech together. As well as measures to counter the pandemic, he seemed concerned with climate change and fitted that item into the Conservative and Johnsonian mantra of "building back better". Railways were to be built, cars and lorries were to be powered by electricity, and at the same time the North of England was to be well and truly fashioned into the Northern Powerhouse that had been heralded by a previous Conservative administration. Four thousand miles of new road was to be built to connect ports and airports with centres of sustainable production. It superficially resembled his paper on undersea cables, with all its connectivity. But its effect on carbon emissions (which were never mentioned) makes it very different.

I am not qualified to write on what is needed on the Humber, Teesside and Tyneside in the North of England, though I do agree that it is good to make that area the hub for constructing wind turbines ready to be placed in the North Sea. But at the end of that section of his speech up popped an item for which I am qualified, so much so that it is worth quoting the whole paragraph from Hansard.

"There is one more road," said Rishi, "I would like to mention: it is one of our most important arteries. It is one of those totemic projects symbolising delay and obstruction. Governments have been trying to fix it since the 1980s. Every year, millions of cars crawl along it in traffic, ruining the backdrop to one of our most historic landmarks. So, to the many Hon. and Right Hon. Members who have campaigned for this moment – the A303: this government is going to get it done." As he came to his climax, rapturous applause and cheers rang out from the government benches. There was just a touch of hubris to this little section of his speech. (Which met its match when a judicial review in July 2021 deemed that the government had not done its homework on the historic landmark – which is, of course, Stonehenge.)

Rishi made this speech only eighteen months after climate change was renamed by many as "climate crisis", after the IPCC published its interim conclusion that the globe's temperature was likely to become critical not at 2 degrees above the level it was in 1800 but at 1.5 degrees. He had artfully dealt with measures he supported to deal with climate change before going on to build back better. And what would be built was road infrastructure, culminating with the A303, all unnecessarily productive of CO_2, both in construction and use.

The A303 had long been a project supported by the Conservatives and indeed by the coalition government. Nick Clegg, when he was leader of the Lib Dems, was one of its most ardent advocates. But because its genesis was in the 1980s, by 2021 it was out of date and Stonehenge was now a World Heritage Site. So much more is now known about the archaeology of Stonehenge – to the very important extent that there is much knowledge of how much more there is to be discovered. And, unlike our Winchester Schools dig at Lankhills fifty years ago where the shadows of graves could be seen in the shiny white of the carefully scraped chalk subsoil, in the Stone Age site at Stonehenge, the discovery of artefacts mostly made of flint and often evidence indicative of early habitation, is usually in the topsoil. Though the projected road would have gone through twin-tunnels, there would have been deep dual-carriage way runnels, in all 2.5 kilometres in length, churning up huge mountains of topsoil before the entrances of the tunnel could be reached. An irony of the new plans compared to the present road was that the latter is popular to tourists and others because the monument can actually be seen, a delight which would no longer exist. Another irony is that the present government, so seemingly determined to follow science and knowledge, was denying us knowledge that is at least as important for our understanding of humans and their ways of living as any plans to inhabit Mars or the moon. As for vehicular traffic on roads, it accounts for some 25 per cent of the UK's emissions of CO_2, which is about the same figure for the emissions from domestic dwellings. Building roads increases emissions both from the act of building (and that's not just building roads but a new more complicated version of cars run on electricity) and from the purpose for which they are built. Emissions will be much more easily lowered by renovating draughty houses or by building much-needed and more sustainable draught-proof houses through a change in the national building regulations. Mankind in the colder parts of the Northern Hemisphere has an existential need to live in a house or flat, but by contrast needs to move around only occasionally. It is quite clear that the priority in a climate crisis is with houses, not roads or airports. The Stonehenge tunnels encapsulate the failure in the mantra of "building back better" properly to analyse which projects are better and which are not. Besides, work on houses employs much more human labour to keep unemployment down; building roads has a preference for machinery like bulldozers, and there is no guarantee that there will be sufficient electricity generated sustainably to power the mass of cars and vans that are envisaged.

Nevertheless, good experimental structures for Research and Development are being built by entrepreneurs, helped out by government money. Nuclear fusion, for example at Aldermaston, or the direct capture of CO_2 in the North of Scotland, or electricity from tide power in the Pentland Firth. Even the new high-speed railway (HS2) could be good. Not every environmentalist thinks so, but there are bound to be projected innovations that are superseded by even better ones. Good too is the construction of wind turbines in the North-East of England, even if the construction of them is by foreign companies often in foreign countries. A huge governmental mistake in early days closed down subsidised local companies in this field and outsourced the work to other countries, with the result that the UK lacks local expertise. The main work is likely to be carried out abroad.

The difficulty, as I see it, is that politicians (and Boris and Rishi are no exceptions) have been so busy constructing their careers, which many people in other professions also do, that they have not had the time nor the inclination to understand climate change. A typical and extremely important illustration of this is the government's reiteration of the claim that the UK has been lowering its carbon footprint (by some 50 per cent) during the last three decades. The UK has done this by outsourcing its manufacturing capabilities to other countries. In reality, because the UK imports so much "stuff" to consume, stuff that we once manufactured, that our carbon footprint has not gone down at all. That is partly because so much that we consume has to be carried from abroad, which encourages the emission of CO2 from cargo boats and aeroplanes. In the end the act of consumption is more important than the act of production, which is encouraged by consumption. The UK hosts at COP26 will have to acknowledge this. Otherwise every nation will be economical with the truth and the gains of COP26, if any, will be viewed as "greenwash".

And so, once again trust is an issue. Boris will have to earn a reputation for trust, a reputation he still does not have. Rishi seems to be more trusted, but as he is very loyal, inevitably he is in tandem with Boris, so that there is a suspicion that his clever, organised mind can paper over the cracks. After all, it was he who stood in for Boris in the party leaders' debates during the 2019 General Election, when Boris not only refused to attend but gave orders to Conservative candidates not to attend hustings on climate change. Obviously too, it has been extremely difficult for government ministers, for reasons quite outside their control during the pandemic, to receive anything more from the thinking public than a grudging trust, with Parliament unable to meet properly at a time when the glare of publicity is intense and the expectation of transparency deeply implanted.

65. Finale, July 2021
(Population – 7.98 billion; CO2 ppm – 415; Centigrade – + 1.19)

In July 2021 a period of extremely hot weather in the UK was ushered in by the patron saint of rain, St. Swithun, once the Bishop of Winchester, whose saint's day is July 15. The day is marked in the Mediterranean by the rising of the Dog Star, Sirius, as it tracks the sun, a malevolent star that sets a month later on the Feast of the Assumption of the Blessed Virgin Mary, or, named more popularly in Italy, Ferragosto. On July 14, Bastille Day commemorates the French Revolution, and thus could be said to be the day of Revolution. If it rains on July 15, on each of the next thirty days at least some rain will fall. On July 15 2021 it did not rain, nor did it in Winchester for the next seven. July 14 did however mark the publication of the first piece of the UK's plan to combat climate change. It dealt with travel; travel by road, plane and sea. Not surprisingly, it concentrated on building, despite the quashing of the A303 tunnel past Stonehenge. But a far more important judicial review of the government's £27 million road programme let those constructions go through.

July was also the month when "Gaia" showed her teeth, frighteningly so. Extreme weather events occurred, in line with the projections of the climate change data – except that these extremes are happening earlier than expected. Extremes? Yes: Extreme Rain in Turkey, in central China, and in Germany (rain not likely to be seen in a hundred years), also in India, Extreme Rain causing Extreme Floods, even in London, and, dare I say, once in Winchester; Extreme Heat, in Canada, in California, in Turkey and in Siberia, causing extreme fires. Extreme? Yes extreme, by as much as 5 degrees Celsius compared to the previous high, causing extreme droughts in Canadian prairies, and elsewhere too: in Madagascar, Ethiopia, Iran, Tibet, etc. And, of course, the ice in the Arctic and in the Antarctic continues to melt, and now is melting faster. And in the final Dog Days of Sirius in the Mediterranean extreme heat and drought caused calamitous fires along the coast of Turkey, through the Aegean Islands, onto the mainland of Greece and at the time of writing to Sicily, Southern Italy, Southern Spain, and Algeria.

This is the state of the planet that the delegations to COP26 in Glasgow have to confront. And with climate change now acknowledged by scientists actually to have arrived, most people who are aware of life outside their own immediate concerns are almost forced to acknowledge it. How to confront it is another matter, indeed the great challenge.

In the midst of all this, I stumbled upon a book almost by chance, written by Dieter Helm, CBE, now Sir Dieter. I met him years ago, in the early nineties, when he was a member of Winchester College's Governing Body. At that time he was a Fellow in Economics at New College Oxford, and as such was a Fellow of Winchester College as laid down in the fourteenth century by William of Wykeham, the College's founder. I attended some of these meetings to give advice on matters to do with Winchester City Council. Dieter always turned up at the porters' gate on his bicycle, presumably because he had put it on the train from Oxford. He did not say much at the meetings I attended, nor did I. But I remember him talking very enthusiastically one day outside in the open air; he was talking about his brilliant team of women researchers who helped him in his drive to understand what was happening to the environment on our planet. It was at about this time (1992) that the first United Nations meeting on climate change was held in Rio.

Later he became the Professor of Economic Policy at Oxford University and I was aware that he was writing a great deal, much of which I found, as I dipped into it, rather too academic. But when Theresa May was prime minister, he came very close to government and wrote the Helm Review on the production of energy in the UK and the great challenges that it faces.

The book that I chanced to find is *NET ZERO: How We Stop Causing Climate Change.*

At the time of writing, that is in August 2021 – one hundred days before COP26 – there is much impatience within the UK Committee on Climate Change (CCC) that no "net zero test" is yet in place for planning decisions; that plans on surface transport, aviation, hydrogen, biomass, and food waste have been delayed (with only transport recently delivered); and that the government, meaning really the prime minister, has made little effort to begin a graduated involvement of the public to know the situation and play its part on climate change. The focus is still totally trained on the pandemic, perhaps not surprisingly. So little has

Boris focussed on climate change that he has delegated responsibility for his part in the crisis leading up to COP26 to Allegra Stratton, the wife of Jamie Forsyth, the editor of *The Spectator* and a school friend of Rishi. Meanwhile not only has Boris disappeared from view on climate change as he did in the General Election of 2019, but the loyal (or over-loyal) Rishi has too. The only visibly active member of the Cabinet on this subject is the ex-airline pilot, Grant Shapps, who flies his own plane and is actually encouraging new airports and unnecessary roads.

It was in the midst of all this when I read Dieter Helm's *NET ZERO*. The centrepiece of his argument is that we have wasted thirty years and billions of pounds, from Rio in 1992 to Glasgow at the end of 2021, by concentrating attention on abolishing CO_2 emissions, which in the meantime have steadily risen at an even faster pace. He particularly aims his scorn at the CCC's report of 2019 which says:

"By reducing emissions produced in the UK to zero, we also end our contribution to rising global temperatures."

Helm goes on to say: "This is misleading in that the net zero target that the CCC advocates is for territorial emissions *in the UK*, and unless every other country we trade with gets to net zero by 2050 too, or we stop importing carbon-intensive goods, it is simply not true. The net zero carbon production target takes no account of the carbon we import *[as a result of outsourcing our manufacturing capacity]* which pervades much of our spending."

In this he is in entire agreement with most ordinary climate change activists who usually try to find the source of what they eat (no beef from Brazil), what they wear (no cheap clothes that include a proportion of plastic), and what they use (no products derived from palm oil or manufactured with the aid of coal or oil). The activists in

Winchester Action on Climate Change have been totally aware for some time that our consumption is fuelling CO_2 emissions abroad and is therefore our responsibility.

And so what is the answer? Dieter Helm's view is that producers of emissions whether in manufacturing or in agriculture are responding to consumer demand. (We should probably forget for the moment that producers often create the demand through the "hidden persuasion" of advertising and herd thinking.) Therefore if consumption is priced, whether in the act of buying or at national borders, the price of carbon-consuming goods will go up and their attraction to both consumer and producers will go down. He recognises that many countries will find this difficult to understand and to put into practice. The UK on the other hand does have a certain amount of awareness and realisation that the existential threat to the human race over the next thirty years is very great. His recommendation, therefore, taking advantage of one aspect of Brexit, is that we should "go it alone" and put a real carbon price on everything that we consume, whether at our borders, or at the individual level. He recognises that this will be painful, but not as painful as the alternative. The UK, as a result, will be able to take some pride in leading the field and other nations will eventually follow.

He recognises that there will still be residual emissions of CO_2. To deal with these, our agricultural practices will have to change, which again as a result of Brexit is more practicable, because we shall be relieved of the polluting practices of the EU's Common Agricultural Policy which encourage industrial methods of farming through excess use of chemical fertilisers and machines. Our new methods will encourage sustainable practices such as rewilding, reforestation, the protection of peat and the prevention from flooding of rivers. These agricultural practices are now largely accepted as the right way forward, partly as the result of Helm's own copious writing on the subject.

I am not in a position to go into an extensive analysis of his theme. I am interested in the welfare of the world's poorest people and nations, about which he says little. It is, however, well known that it is the poorest countries which suffer most from global warming, a warming almost entirely produced by rich countries and particularly by their richest people. It, therefore, has to stop. The logic of the UK putting a price on carbon at its borders must lead to poorer countries looking after their own peoples, by using native resources for their own purposes and not for foreign consumption, whether it be runner beans from Kenya, avocados from Chile, or cotton in the form of throwaway garments from Bangladesh.

A big question remains. Have we enough time to make that transition work? Or, indeed, have we enough time at all? The USA, according to John Kerry, its Climate Envoy, seems to be bent on big Developments resulting from Research to build its way out of trouble with no mention of a change in people's habits. The UK seems to be following suit. Because it was possible, the thinking goes, to put men on the moon within ten years of the policy being announced in the fifties, surely it is possible to follow the same route in combatting climate change? But is that really possible, when the objective is much wider and when the competitor is not the USSR but Nature? Won't it be the case that, with the basic transitions having to take place before 2030, a seemingly indiscriminate policy of big development and "building back better" is likely to aggravate the very causes of climate change? And so is it really sensible, when we are already experiencing the first results of climate change and scientists are saying that the change is happening more quickly and that tipping points are more likely to arrive sooner than expected? Even now ice, which reflects heat away from the planet, is disappearing faster from the Arctic. And the dark sea, soon to be revealed, will by contrast rapidly absorb that heat.

66 Envoi

This book is ending on a dark note. By the time it is published (if it ever is), much more will be known, knowledge that may be more hopeful or maybe not. But this book acts as a kind of record of where we are in the summer of 2021. We are only at the start of "the canyon"; and the chaos and hardship are already huge, amplified by the speed at which news rushes round the world. Two thousand and fifty years ago the Roman poet Vergil died leaving his great epic, *The Aeneid*, unfinished. He wanted it destroyed but the emperor Augustus insisted that it should be published. One of its most famous lines runs thus:

"*Sunt lacrimae rerum et mentem mortalia tangunt*"

It is an extraordinarily difficult line to translate; it is full of allusion and implication, but it could go thus: "The World is Full of Tears and the Mortality of Everything Infects the Soul." When we think of Afghanistan, the favelas, the Sub-Sahel, the homelessness, immigrants escaping war, drought and flood, the vast gap between rich and poor, the disappearance of trees, the disappearance of species, the drying up of grasses, and the sheer ignorance and irresponsibility of Mankind, it is hard not to weep. Yet, even the tears, like failed monsoons, are dry.

After the death of the Duke of Edinburgh and before his funeral at Windsor, I was dotting 'i's and crossing 't's in this book before sending it to a literary agent. I am not a royalist, nor am I against the royals. I accept the situation. But to someone of my age and background the Queen and the Duke have had a defining role in life. I heard their wedding broadcast on the wireless in my first year at Belhaven. I saw the Coronation in my first year at Glenalmond. I was delighted that the first ascent of Mount Everest in the Himalayas was somehow connected to the royal event. The Queen and the Duke formed a glamorous couple and for a boy of fourteen she was an icon. And over a period of seventy years they have presided over the UK's version of "Gibbon's Years".

And so, it was natural for Jane and me to sit on our sofa with curtains drawn to watch the Royal funeral on our home cinema provided by the BBC. Outside, it was a dazzlingly sunny, cold spring day for the enactment of the ceremonial parade. Jane with her naval background wanted to watch all the pageantry; I was more concerned with the service in the Royal Chapel. I saw some of the pageantry shown by cameras placed high above the open spaces. The military men and women, brightly dressed in their colourful uniforms and strange attire, their faces half obscured by black pandemic masks, were all marching and manoeuvring in time, up and down.

It suddenly struck me: on our little television screen they looked like puppets.

Then, in the huge empty chapel, once the small royal congregation was seated almost invisibly, its hugeness and emptiness took over my mind. At a time of an unpitying pandemic and before the chaos that is coming, this place and ceremony reminded me of that empty ritual cenotaph in Winchester, excavated fifty years ago, but carefully laid out 1,600 years ago in the final spasms of the Western Roman Empire.

APPENDIX i: Bibliography

Here is a list of the books that have contributed to the main theme of this book and to which I have referred. The list is in the chronological order in which I read them. Some of the books I read long ago, and at this end of my life I am not in the right place to include academic references to pages and paragraphs.

Vance Packard: The Hidden Persuaders (1957)
Vance Packard: The Waste Makers (1960)
Rachel Carson: Silent Spring (1962)
Barbara Ward and René Dubos: Only One Earth: The Care and Maintenance of a Small Planet (1972)
E. F. Schumacher: Small is Beautiful (1973)
John V. Taylor: Enough is Enough (1975)
W. K. C. Guthrie: The Greeks and their Gods (1950)
Derek and Julia Parker: The Compleat Astrologer (1971)
Sir Michael Tippett: Moving into Aquarius (1959)
Sir Bernard Lovell: In the Centre of Immensities (1979)
The Brandt Report: North–South: A programme for Survival (1980)
Giles Clarke: The Roman Cemetery at Lankhills (Winchester

Studies, 3.ii, Ed. Martin Biddle) (1979)

Jonathon Porritt: Seeing Green (1984)

David Pepper: Modern Environmentalism (1996)

Richard D. North: Life on a Modern Planet (1996)

Bjorn Lomborg: The Skeptical Environmentalist (2001)

Fred Pearce: The Last Generation (2006)

Professor David J. C. MacKay: Sustainable Energy without the Hot Air (2006)

James Martin: The Meaning of the 21st Century (2006)

James Lovelock: The Revenge of Gaia (2006)

Nicholas Stern: The Stern Report (2006)

Bryan Ward-Perkins: The Fall of Rome and the End of Civilisation (2005)

Nigel Lawson: An Appeal to Reason – A Cool Look at Global Warming (2008)

Ian Plimer: Heaven and Earth (2009)

Christian Gerondeau: The Great Delusion (2010)

Paul Booth et al: The Late Roman Cemetery at Lankhills, Winchester – Excavations 2000–2005 (Oxford Archaeology, Monograph 10) (2010)

Michael E. Mann: The Hockey Stick and the Climate Wars (2012)

Bill McGuire: Waking the Giant – How a Changing Climate Triggers Earthquakes, Tsunamis, and Volcanoes (2012)

Naomi Klein: This Changes Everything – Capitalism vs the Climate (2014)

Christophe Bonneuil & Jean Baptiste Fressoz: The Shock of the Anthropocene (2016)

Kate Raworth: Doughnut Economics: Seven ways to think like a 21st century economist (2017)

Caroline M. Stuckert (Ed.): The People of Early Winchester (Winchester Studies, 9.i Gen. Ed. Martin Biddle) (2017)

Pope Francis: Let Us Dream (2020)

Mariana Mazzucato: The Value of Everything – Making and Taking in the Global Economy (2018)

Michael Ashcroft: Going for Broke – The Rise of Rishi Sunak (2020)

Tom Bower: Boris Johnson – The Gambler (2020)

Professor Dieter Helm: Net Zero: How We Stop Causing Climate Change (2020)

APPENDIX ii. Dramatis Personae

I am aware that there are many names in this book. I do not apologise. Everyone's name defines them and well-known names help a reader to imagine the scene. Occasionally I do not give a name, partly to avoid an overload. Some names are in the public domain and here I give the barest of information on them if it is not included in the text.

The two villages
San Michele: The Carpinelli Families – Tito with *Aria, Ave, and Alberto*; Corrado and Ginevra with *Roberto, Ivana, Francesca and Giuseppe*; *Elio and Stefania*. **The Teodori family** – Gianni with Maria, and six children. **The Menichetti Family** – Ugo and Maria, with six children. **Augu Calanca** and his mother. **Il Conte** and **La Contessa Bulgarini** with Gheri and Monica.

Sermugnano: The Centoscudi families – Lillo and Gabriela, with Loris and Donatella (Giuseppe and Francesca) also Marco with Alina (Dennis), also Monia and Fabrizio (Gabriele and Bianca); Giuliano and Franca with Manuela and Maurizio; Silvano. **Livia and Navino** in the shop; **Augusto** nicknamed L' Imperatore; **Andrea** and **Joanna** with tourist buses; **Marcello**, the village builder.

Winchester College
Sir Desmond Lee, Headmaster, Cambridge philosophy and classics don, previously Head of Clifton College; **Roger Montgomery**, Talented mathematician, co-author of the advanced book in the schools' mathematics project of the 1960s, brother of **Shirley Marro**, chatelaine of Château de Fosseuse;

Mark Stephenson, Inspirational tutor to many renowned academic historians. **Count Nicolas Sollohub**, Russian tutor and lecturer at the Royal Naval College, Dartmouth before coming to Winchester. **Bunny Dowdeswell**, author in the Nuffield Science Project of the 1960s and later Professor of Biology at Bath University; **Richard Bass,** thoughtful, far-sighted housemaster of DuBoulay's; **Peter Partner**, journalist, historian, author of *The Lands of St. Peter;* **Johnnie Stow**, Housemaster, Head of Classics; **Kenneth Kettle,** Housemaster, Modern Linguist; *David Smith, Chemist, Housemaster, Italophile;* **Michael St. John Parker,** Head of History, Head of Abingdon School; **Paul Bates**, School Chaplain; **James Miller**, Housemaster, Head of Economics, District Councillor, Headships of Framlingham College & Royal Grammar School, Newcastle; **John Falconer**, classicist, expert sleuth of stolen Greek vases, civil servant in the EU, musician; **Rev. Robert Ferguson**, School Chaplain.

Pupils Taught – mentioned here
Dr. Timothy Wilson, Keeper of Western Art, Ashmolean Museum, Professor of Western Renaissance Art, Oxford University; **Dr. Iain McGilchrist,** All Souls Fellow in Literature and Medicine, Polymath, Author of *The Master and his Emissary: The Divided Brain and the Making of the Western World;* **Nigel McGilchrist,** Art Historian, lecturer in American Universities, author of *McGilchrist's Greek Islands;* **Rishi Sunak,** Chancellor of the Exchequer, 2020–2022

Wardens of Winchester College mentioned
Sir Anthony Tuke, Chairman of Barclay's Bank 1951– 62, Warden 1964–70; **Lord Aldington (Sir Toby Low),** Conservative MP, Distinguished military service WW2, Chairman of Grindley's Bank, Warden 1983–90; **Sir**

Jeremy Morse, Exec. Director, Bank of England, Chairman of Lloyd's Bank, Chancellor of Bristol University, Warden 1990–1998.

Winchester City Council
Councillors: Georgie Busher (Leader, Conservative), **Pat Edwards** (Planning, Conservative), **Brian Collins** (Health & Works, Liberal Democrat), **George Fothergill** (Amenities, Liberal Democrat), **John Cloyne** (Housing, Labour). **Officers: David Cowan** (CEO), **Noel Mullins** (Housing), **Andrew Clark** (Housing Finance), **David Marklew** (Traffic & Engineering).

Others
Magnus Linklater, CBE, journalist, political writer, Scottish savant; **Allan Massie, CBE,** political journalist, sports writer, novelist; **Sir Bruce Pattullo, CBE,** Governor of the Bank of Scotland, Trustee of Hertford College, Oxford; **Ken Bartlett, CBE,** Finance Director, Housing Corporation; **Adam Raphael,** political Journalist and writer; **Willie Abrahams,** The mind of Africa, Nkrumah; University of California, USA; **Sir David Calcutt,** barrister, inquiries, Master of Magdalene College, Cambridge. **Professor Sir Dieter Helm CBE,** Professor of Economic Policy, Oxford University, Fellow in Economics, New College Oxon.

ACKNOWLEDGEMENTS

My sister, Joan Mary, wrote a memoir, "The Old Tin Trunk", on her early life, which is the source for the section on Pre-Consciousness. Felicity Calderari, in our twenty-seven years together, was naturally attuned to the needs of climate change through her interest in simple Italian living. Jane Alexander, in the years we have known each other and lived together, has taught me much about myself and in general the needs of the human psyche in a rapidly changing world. Winchester College, my employer for thirty-seven years, gave me wonderful space over and above the teaching for public exams to examine what life is about and learn from the acumen of many pupils and my colleagues. In the process of producing this book I am indebted to Paul Williams for a very simple solution to pulling it together. My colleague, John Falconer, has been a great supporter. Even more am I indebted to Matthew Huntly of P & G Wells for steering me away from too much data and giving me much encouraging and wise advice. And in the past a big thank-you to my parents, Harry and Laurina, who at a difficult time for them and the UK saw me safely and enjoyably through my own school years and encouraged my love for the natural world. Others who have encouraged this book to see the light of day: Will Martin who read it and liked it, Wendell Harris and Christine Smith, and David and Penny Kempton, whose lively conversation helped to prevent too many versions of the Epilogue being torn up. I also want to thank the members of Matador, who, as Socrates might have put it, were the cheerful and patient midwives to the book: Hannah Dakin, Sophie Morgan, Fern Bushnell, Hayley Russell, and the copy editor, Imogen Palmer. Finally, I would like to thank Kath Rudge, artist, teacher and my niece, who jumped at the idea of producing a book cover, which is both beautiful and symbolic.

EPILOGUE, 16 May 2022

The twenty-first century began with the terrorist attacks on the twin towers of the World Trade Center in New York and the Pentagon in Washington. Thus was started an epidemic of urban destruction: in Baghdad and Iraq, in Gaza, in Aleppo and Syria, and now in 2022 in Ukraine. Russia has taken these assaults to a new level, and the outlook for getting to grips with the climate crisis has become considerably more murky.

Quite apart from the terrible human suffering, the carbon cost of rebuilding vast areas of destruction will be significant. Even more important are questions about the fitness and ability of human leaders to recognise what is likely to happen to humanity as a whole. The main adversary to be faced is no longer human competition, but Mother Nature herself of which humanity is just a part. In his lofty defence of Mother Russia President Putin forgets entirely that Mother Russia is much dependent on Mother Nature.

There is also the question of lies and deception. With his Special Military Operation Putin has bound the Russian people to a falsehood. Dealing with the climate crisis needs clarity of both vision and explanation of that clear vision. Unfortunately Putin is not the only villain here. The Covid pandemic gained traction because both the Chinese government and President Trump were, at best, economical with the truth and at the worst denied it as fake news. And our own Prime Minister makes promises with no sufficiently clear idea on how to keep them, and, it seems, covers his inadequacies with what seem to be lies even in the House of Commons.

Telling lies and waging war are addictive pursuits. Boris Johnson's whole Churchillian mindset, nurtured since his schooldays, makes it much easier for him and his self-worth to wage a good war than to confront the climate crisis.

In short, this terrible war is a terrible distraction. It does, of course, need to be fought, and it has thrown up one excellent leader, a man of parts, untainted it seems by the lure of greatness. I mean, of course, Volodymyr Zelensky.

In the meantime extremes of weather are becoming worse and more frequent. Kabul has fallen and Afghan women are back in burqas. There is a food crisis in poorer parts of the world, and even in the UK, because the export of wheat from Ukraine, along with many other commodities, is blocked. Some non-national corporations, businesses, and private individuals are beginning to make progress on the climate crisis, but the vital rapidity of action that is required now needs clear-sighted vision from the world's most influential political leaders.

On that note I must stop.